CONGRESS

KEYSTONE OF THE WASHINGTON ESTABLISHMENT

CONGRESS.
KEYSTONE OF THE
WASHINGTON ESTABLISHMENT

MORRIS P. FIORINA

NEW HAVEN AND LONDON
YALE UNIVERSITY PRESS 1977

Designed by Sally Sullivan
and set in Press Roman type.
Printed in the United States of America by
Vail-Ballou Press, Binghamton, N.Y.

Published in Great Britain, Europe, Africa, and
Asia (except Japan) by Yale University Press,
Ltd., London. Distributed in Latin America by
Kaiman & Polon, Inc., New York City; in
Australia and New Zealand by Book & Film
Services, Artarmon, N.S.W., Australia; and in
Japan by Harper & Row, Publishers, Tokyo
Office.

Library of Congress Cataloging in Publication Data

Fiorina, Morris P
  Congress, keystone of the Washington establishment.

  (A Yale fastback ; 18)
  Includes index.
  1. United States.   Congress.   2. Administrative
agencies—United States.   3. Representative
government and representation—United States.
I. Title.
JK1071.F55   328.73   76-54606
ISBN 0-300-02132-1
ISBN 0-300-02125-9 pbk.

TO MY PARENTS —

HELEN & MO

Contents

Figures and Tables

Figures

Tables

Acknowledgments

A number of people contributed in a variety of ways to the writing of this book. My distinguished colleague John Ferejohn fanned the flames of my interest by impishly pointing out that recent trends in congressional elections were inconsistent with aspects of my earlier published work. My curiosity aroused, I prevailed upon the Division of the Humanities and Social Sciences at Caltech to fund the field trip described in chapter 4, although I could provide justification little more concrete than a hunch that I could learn something by going into the field. Another colleague, Charles Plott, encouraged me to communicate my developing ideas to a broad audience rather than bury them in the pages of specialized journals. These individuals and institutions got me going. My secretary, Georgeia Hutchinson, kept me going. Her rapid and steady pace prevented me from slacking off in the home stretch.

Numerous individuals read and commented on the manuscript. My wife, Mary, and my good friends Rick and Merry Rossini flagged passages and tables that were incomprehensible to the nonspecialist. Graduate students Randy Calvert, Paul Thomas, and Barry Weingast egged me on, as did colleague Roger Noll. Other colleagues—John Aldrich, Herbert Asher, Robert Bates, Ken Shepsle, and Herbert Weisberg—reacted to my ideas, some more positively than others. (Bates, incidentally, rendered the valuable service of introducing me to the good people of Yale University Press.) Finally, day-to-day interaction with Burt Klein and Mel Hinich has affected my outlook in various ways. As usual, however, I absolve all of the above-named individuals of any direct responsibility for what ultimately appears on the pages that follow. Presumably they will privately claim credit for any ideas that gain general acceptance.

Once again I thank my lovely wife, Mary, who again receives any royalties this book earns. Her expectations are lower this time around.

CONGRESS

KEYSTONE OF THE WASHINGTON ESTABLISHMENT

Introduction

The presidential campaigns of 1976 offered a curious spectacle: serious candidates for national office ran *for* Washington office by running *against* Washington.[1] They asked us to believe that the seat of national government is (choose): (a) immobile, (b) corrupt, (c) dangerously out of touch, (d) all of the above. The critics charged that the country is misgoverned by a Washington establishment, a Washington inner circle, or a group of Washington insiders. Such charges apparently carried a ring of truth; even Gerald Ford— twenty-eight years a member of the ruling circles—could not resist the temptation to attack Washington.

Wild charges fly in every election year of course. The theme that the government is wrongfully influenced by an unrepresentative, illegitimate, or even conspiratorial group surfaces quite regularly in American political campaigns. The Washington establishment can be viewed as a contemporary successor to the Slave Power, Wall Street, Merchants of Death, Malefactors of Great Wealth, the International Communist Conspiracy, and the Military Industrial Complex. Those seeking political power regularly create and use such symbols as elements of campaign strategy. But why should they do so unless such strategies periodically succeed? And why should conspiratorial symbols succeed unless candidates and others can marshal evidence consistent with some notion of inner circle rule?[2] And how can anyone offer generally convincing evidence unless at least a semblance of such inner circle rule exists? The concept of an international communist conspiracy never attained widespread credibility, rightfully so, and that notion now sits in the dustbin of political history. But candidates could and did persuade a large part of the electorate of the existence of a slave power, and a new party rode that issue to control of the national government. I humbly suggest that the Republicans' success of a century ago stemmed in no small part from the veracity of their charges.

This book makes a simple argument: the notion of a Washington establishment should not be dismissed as just another campaign slogan, a discomforting ghost conjured up by Ronald Reagan and Jimmy Carter in order to scare voters away from U.S. senators with presidential fever. I am convinced that something meriting the name of Washington establishment exists and that its continued operation has potentially disturbing implications for the future welfare of this country. I have written this short book in the hope of stimulating serious investigation and discussion of the workings of the Washington establishment. Otherwise the situation might escape the limelight once the heat of the campaign diminishes.

I have not written a topical work before, and it is with some uncertainty that I do so now: topical writing arouses suspicion in serious academic circles (although few serious academics decline the opportunity when it is urged upon them). I have written this book on a level midway between academic and lay audiences. On the one hand, the book is more systematic and more thoroughly documented than the typical "pop" book on politics. On the other hand, parts of the book are more theoretical (i.e. speculative) than the typical academic study of Congress. Chapters 1–3 build on a firm foundation of academic research, but the remainder of the book relies more on examples and on the intuitive plausibility of the argument than on exhaustive data analyses.

The book differs from academic studies of Congress in one other major respect: its tone is openly critical. My fellow congressional scholars have written exhaustively about the positive aspects of our national legislature. Much of what they have written I agree with. But I believe that they have been less thorough in analyzing the negative side of Congress. I trust that one avowedly critical effort will not destroy the balance.

The plan of the book is somewhat circuitous. I will ask the reader to follow me along an intellectual and physical path that begins with a question bearing no apparent relation to the existence of a Washington establishment. I followed this path to that conclusion, and I hope to convince the reader to do likewise. Before proceeding, let me equip the reader with a summary description of what lies at the end of our path.

There is a Washington establishment. In fact, it is a hydra with each head only marginally concerned with the others' existence. These establishments are *not* malevolent, centrally directed conspiracies against the American people. Rather, they are unconsciously evolved and evolving networks of congressmen, bureaucrats, and organized subgroups of the citizenry all seeking to achieve their own goals. Contrary to what is popularly believed, the bureaucrats are not the problem. Congressmen are. *The Congress is the key to the Washington establishment.* The Congress created the establishment, sustains it, and most likely will continue to sustain and even expand it. But I emphasize again that the disturbing aspects of the Washington establishment follow from the uncoordinated operations of the overall system, not from any sinister motivation of those who compose it. The perceptive observer can identify the actors, specify their motives, and analyze their methods of operation. But many of those in the heart of the establishment are genuinely unaware that they are members in good standing.

DOONESBURY

by Garry Trudeau

Chapter 1
The Case of the Vanishing Marginals
(with apologies to David Mayhew)

Throughout the postwar period we have heard jokes about the length of congressional careers. Most of these come in connection with discussions of the congressional seniority system, which purportedly elevates ancient southern congressmen to chairmanships of the standing committees of Congress.[1] Behind the jokes there stand hard facts. Congress today is occupied by career politicians. Generally speaking the only congressmen who do not intend to spend the rest of their careers in Congress are those senators who hope to move up to the presidency. Since World War II nearly 90 percent of all incumbents have sought reelection in any given election, and approximately 90 percent of all those who ran were successful.[2] There have been exceptions of course. The elections of 1958, 1964, and 1974 were a bit rougher on incumbents than usual. And voluntary retirement rates jumped in the early 1970s under the stimulus of significant improvements in congressional pensions and the unpleasantries of holding office during the Watergate period. But despite this recent infusion of fresh blood, we have every reason to believe that the new congressmen intend to match the careers of the older ones they replaced.

The professionalization of Congress is a twentieth-century phenomenon.[3] During the nineteenth century congressional turnover consistently amounted to 40–50 percent of the membership at each election, sometimes going even higher (73 percent in 1843, 61 percent in 1853, 58 percent in 1875). Not until the turn of the century did the average continuous service of congressmen climb to five years. The seniority system itself postdates the 1909–11 revolt in the House, although it arose somewhat earlier in the Senate. In an era in which congressmen had no seniority, the system made no sense.

What factors transformed the unstable Congress of the nineteenth century into the professionalized Congress of the twentieth? A variety of influences have been identified. The realignment of the 1890s effectively ended two-party competition in many areas of the country, particularly the South, but in parts of the North and Midwest as well. Fewer congressmen went down to defeat under these conditions. But there was also a large voluntary component to the change. During the early nineteenth century, Washington was a provincial rural village set off in a swampy river bottom. Congressmen regularly abandoned their posts for the more pleasant conditions of public office in the relatively more cosmopolitan state capitals.[4] Sometimes congressmen had to leave office to repair their personal finances—Congress was a penurious body in those days (with good reason: congressional turnover rose 15 percent following a pay raise in 1816). In the home districts the congressional nomination was sometimes viewed as an honor to be spread among the good citizens of the district. Abraham Lincoln, for example, was denied renomination to Congress; he had already had his turn.

As the nineteenth century passed, conditions changed. The power and significance of the national government increased steadily, particularly following the Civil War. By 1890 it was no longer true that the Virginia State Legislature was more important than the U.S. Congress. The typical congressman had relatively fewer attractive career opportunities outside Washington. Facing these changed conditions, he responded by more frequent attempts to attain reelection and, not at all incidentally, to gain a greater degree of control over his destiny. The 1910 revolt, from which followed the contemporary seniority system, can be interpreted as an attempt by the rank and file to reduce the uncertainty surrounding a congressional career.[5] By breaking the arbitrary power of the party leadership and substituting an automatic leadership selection system, individual congressmen could plan a congressional career in a manner not previously possible. Seniority, in turn, interacted with congressional turnover. A congressman could no longer take periodic leaves of office to repair his finances or just to vacation. To do so would be to forfeit his seniority. District political elites could no longer afford to rotate the congressional nomination. Such practices would penalize their districts within the congressional power structure. The longer a congressman stayed in Washington, the greater his incentive to stay longer. The seniority system is misunderstood. Its principal effect is not that it selects old and unrepresentative congressmen to chair the committees; the system encourages old and unrepresentative congressmen generally and deprives local districts of any incentive to replace them with younger, more qualified, and more representative individuals.

The preceding discussion provides some general background on the Congress and how it has developed over time. Let us now examine some developments that have occurred more recently and over a time span measured in decades, not centuries.

Between 1940 and 1970 congressional turnover continued to decline, although the change was slight compared to what had already occurred. During this period turnover declined from about one-fourth of the members of the House to about one-sixth, even slipping below 10 percent in the election of 1968. (In 1974 turnover was comparatively high, 21 percent, but this figure was lower than that recorded in nine of ten elections between 1930 and 1950. And in 1976, turnover dropped back to about 15 percent.) What accounts for this contemporary decline? Changes in the congressional context offer no clues, and the increasing congressional membership stability occurs at a time when the electorate is growing increasingly volatile at the presidential level.

The key to this small puzzle was provided by Professor David Mayhew in an article subtitled "The Case of the Vanishing Marginals."[6] Political scientists traditionally use the term "marginal" district to refer to those congressional districts not firmly in the camp of one party or the other. "Swing" district is another commonly used term. "Safe" districts, of course, are those which are not marginal. Customarily, marginal districts are identified by victory percentages of 50–55 percent. In this range a particularly strong effort by a challenger, a weak effort by the incumbent, or a national swing against the incumbent's party may be enough to swing the district from one party's camp into the other's. In the recent past marginal districts have accounted for the bulk of the change in the membership in Congress—national swings such as those occurring in 1946 and 1964 exact a high toll in congressmen from such districts.

Mayhew's important observation was a simple one: the marginal district is going the way of the passenger pigeon.

In figure 1 I have excerpted some of Mayhew's data. The left-hand graphs record the percentage of the vote attained by Democratic congressional candidates in each of the congressional districts contested by an incumbent. To read the 1948 graph, for example, in 15 percent of the districts the Democratic candidate got 45–50 percent of the vote, in 12 percent of the districts he received 50–55 percent of the vote, in 15 percent of the districts he received 95–100 percent of the vote (mostly uncontested southern districts), etc. The proportion of marginal districts, of course, is given by the height of the bars in the middle of the graph in the area of 50 percent Democratic. In the right-hand graphs the presidential vote by congressional district appears for (later) comparative purposes.

When we look through the series of figures constructed by Mayhew, what do we find? In 1948 most of the districts fall in the competitive range. Ignoring the uncontested districts, as we depart further and further from a 50–50 split we find fewer and fewer congressional districts. In 1956 the distribution is a bit more ragged and asymmetric, but the overall picture is largely the same. In the 1960s, however, changes are clearly evident. A trough appears in the area of a 50–50 split in 1962 and becomes quite pronounced by 1966. It is as if someone had stepped on the 1948 distribution, depressing the middle and swelling the ends.

By the 1970s the bimodality has become strikingly clear. Fewer and fewer districts fall in the swing or marginal range. More and more fall in the range that is quite comfortable—safe—for congressional incumbents. In 1972 fewer than 25 percent of the incumbents who ran won by less than a 60–40 margin. Using our 55 percent rule of thumb, 90 percent of all 1972 winners would be classified as safe, whereas only 75 percent would have been similarly classified following the 1948 election.[7]

Seldom in the social sciences do data speak so clearly. Mayhew's figures provide us with a partial answer: congressional turnover has

Figure 1. Congressional Vote in Districts with Incumbents Running, 1948–1972

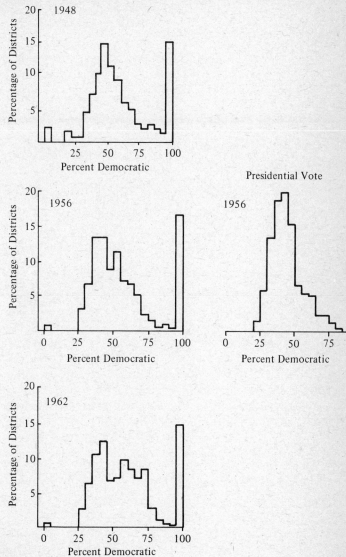

Figure 1–*Continued*

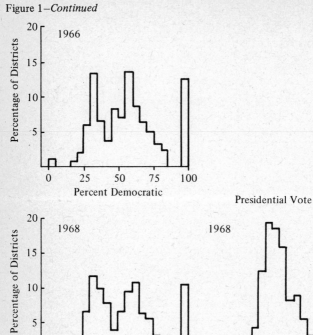

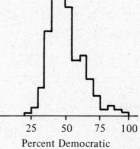

Presidential Vote

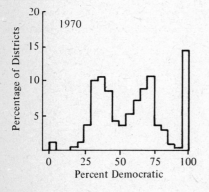

Figure 1–*Continued*

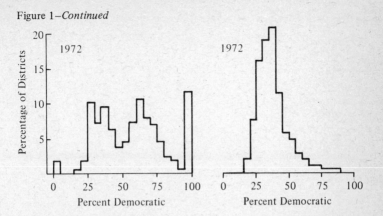

Source: The 1956 to 1972 data are drawn from David Mayhew, "Congressional Elections: The Case of the Vanishing Marginals," *Polity* 6 (1974): 295–317. The 1948 data are drawn from the 1948 *Congressional Quarterly Almanac* and the Congressional Quarterly *Guide to U.S. Elections.*

declined in the postwar period because the kind of district that produces the lion's share of that turnover is disappearing. This partial answer, however, raises two additional questions. First, why are the marginal districts disappearing? Second, why should anyone care? Answering the first question starts us down the path that leads to the Washington establishment. Answering the second provides the motivation to follow that path. So, let us briefly consider the significance of marginal districts before returning to the main lines of the analysis.

Chapter 2
The Marginal District: Some Brief
Remarks about the Victim

Upon casual consideration of the lot of a marginal district congressman, we are likely to feel a touch of sympathy. Here is a would-be statesman elected by 52 or 53 percent of the vote who lives in mortal fear for his political life. One mistake on a roll-call vote, one slip of the tongue, one touch of scandal, an unpopular presidential candidate put forward by his party or a popular one by the opposition—any such factor might return him to the law office in the county seat. He lives insecurely with the knowledge that ambitious members of both district parties savor his electoral weakness and impatiently await any small signal that this is *the time* to take him on.

Our initial sympathetic reaction is probably a mistake, however. The marginal congressman is analogous to the rabbit in a natural ecosystem: his life is hard in a world full of coyotes, but he's necessary for the health of the overall system.

The marginal congressman provides the means by which changes in popular sentiments receive expression in the halls of the Capitol.[1] Safe district congressmen come and stay (until voluntary retirement or moral indiscretion opens up their seat). An electoral debacle on the part of their party's presidential candidate might depress their percentage of the vote from 65 to 60 percent. An all-out challenge within the district might do likewise. But generally speaking the safe congressman observes the ebb and flow of political debate in the country as something of an uninvolved observer. Popular wisdom portrays the congressman as weak and vacillating, one who sways with every political breeze. But academic studies suggest to the contrary that incumbent congressmen maintain a marked stability in their positions over time.[2] If you wish to know how a congressman is voting in 1970, the chances are very good that his 1960 voting record will tell you. *As a consequence, the only reliable way to achieve policy change in Congress is to change congressmen.* And here the marginal district enters.

The existence of marginal districts builds necessary responsiveness into the electoral system. Whether coming to Washington on the coattails of a popular president (1964) or over the bodies of the congressional victims of an unpopular one (1974), the marginal district congressmen constitute the electoral mandate. Consider, for example, some data on the comparative voting records of the 1964 marginal congressmen and those whom they defeated (37 districts were involved):[3]

Average Decrease in Conservative Coalition Support   61%
Average Increase in Support for a Larger Federal Role   51%

The Conservative Coalition Support Score is a general measure of conservatism based on all those votes in which Republicans and southern Democrats coalesce against northern Democrats. The Larger Federal Role Support Score is a generalized Liberalism Score. (Both of these scores are compiled by *Congressional Quarterly*, an independent research organization.) Clearly the new congressmen, almost all of whom were Democrats, voted in dramatically different fashion from the congressmen they defeated. On the average they were 61 percent less supportive of the conservative coalition and 51 percent more supportive of federal intervention in society than those whom they replaced. One may credit the political leadership of Lyndon Johnson for the legislation passed by the 89th Congress, but one should not forget the replacement of a significant number of conservative Republicans by liberal Democrats. The importance of those votes is apparent when we consider the differences between the voting records of marginal Republicans and those whom they defeated in 1966 (29 districts were involved):

Average Increase in Conservative Coalition Support   58%
Average Decrease in Support for a Larger Federal Role   43%

Undoubtedly, Johnson was a less effective leader in the 90th Congress. But he also had thirty fewer liberals and thirty more conservatives to try to lead.

The significance of the marginal district is clear in any discussion of electoral mandates. Even on a smaller scale, though, the importance of the marginals should not be ignored. Those in a district who are dissatisfied with their congressman must beat him, not persuade him. And they have a chance only in a marginal district. *As such districts disappear we face the possibility of a Congress composed of professional officeholders oblivious to the changing political sentiments of the country.*

Of course we must be careful not to treat the distinction between marginal and safe districts as something ordained by God. Why are some districts marginal and others not? The traditional explanation is based on the relative socioeconomic homogeneity or heterogeneity of the district.[4] A black central city district is not likely to have a healthy Republican organization. Nor is a WASP, small townish New England or midwestern district likely to have a flourishing Democratic party. Marginal districts have tended to be those whose socioeconomic structure provides a base for both parties—an agricultural area containing a medium-sized industrial city, a district originally settled by New England pietists and later invaded by Lutherans and Catholics, a metropolitan district containing both wealthy suburbs and ethnic blue-collar neighborhoods. Some politically relevant social or economic cleavage that divides the district into relatively equal parts has been viewed as a necessary condition for a district to fall into the marginal class.

Within the boundaries set by socioeconomic conditions, individual congressmen may of course take actions that advance or impair their electoral fortunes. A basically marginal district might appear safe when held by some particularly effective incumbent, just as a basically safe district might appear marginal when held by some particularly ineffective one. Congressmen are not passive, powerless robots randomly selected from the district's population. Thus the disappearance of the marginals suggests that we examine two factors: (1) possible changes in the socioeconomic homogeneity of congressional districts, (2) possible changes in the effectiveness of congressional incumbents. In the next chapter we will consider the first possibility and reject it. In later chapters we will see how incumbents have managed to structure Washington influence relationships so as to make their reelections ever more certain.

Chapter 3
The Vanishing Marginals: Who Done It?

Is there any basis for arguing that the disappearance of the marginals stems from the increasing socioeconomic homogeneity of congressional districts? On the face of it the charge is dubious. Socioeconomic change tends to be gradual; it takes decades to show up. The decline of the marginals, however, has been fairly rapid. In the late 1950s everything looked normal. By 1970 something had happened.

Could it be that socioeconomic cleavage lines have become less politically relevant? Again, the suggestion is doubtful. Dormant religious differences were awakened in 1960. The New Deal class cleavages were sharpened and reinforced in the 1964 election. Race came to the fore during all the mid-sixties elections. If anything, socioeconomic cleavages became more politically relevant during the 1960s.[1]

A more sophisticated argument relies on the observation that congressional districts do not just "happen" to be more or less homogeneous in a socioeconomic sense. Rather, a district's characteristics in some part depend on the actions of the state legislature, which draws the district's boundaries. Within limits, the state legislature can choose how homogeneous and therefore how competitive its congressional districts will be. Consider a hypothetical state of one thousand voters, half of whom are blue-collar workers who typically vote for the alpha party, half of whom are white-collar workers who typically vote for the omega party. If the voters are mixed evenly throughout the state's population, any drawing of district boundaries would produce closely divided (marginal) districts. But suppose that the blue-collar workers live together in the northern half of the state, while the white-collar workers live together in the southern half of the state. In this case the state legislature has a great deal of influence on the shape of the state's congressional elections. Assume the state is to be divided into ten districts of equal population which meet the modern requirements of contiguity and compactness. Then the legislature could draw congressional districts lines vertically (north to south) and produce ten marginal districts each containing 50 percent alpha voters (in the northern half) and 50 percent omega voters (in the southern half). (See the first diagram.) But on the other hand, the legislature could just as easily draw the district boundaries horizontally, thereby producing ten safe districts, five containing only alpha voters, five containing only omega voters. (See the second diagram.) Clearly, if this hypothetical state were to change its districting arrangement from the first case to the second, ten marginals would disappear.

To be sure, the conditions of our hypothetical example are not fully met in the real world. Groups are not monolithic in their political allegiances, nor do they congregate in ethnically or otherwise pure regions. But groups do have political leanings, and their members do tend to live together rather than to mix randomly in the population. Thus legislatures can exert great influence on the shape of the state's congressional elections, although not absolute influence as in the hypothetical example.

Considerations like the preceding suggest the hypothesis that changed redistricting strategies have reduced the number of marginal districts. The U.S. Supreme Court's "one man, one vote" decisions directly stimulated widespread redistricting during the mid to late 1960s.[2] Some political scientists trace the decline of the marginals directly to the court-ordered redistrictings. Professor Edward Tufte, for example, refers to the latter as "incumbent protection acts."[3]

District

1	2	3	4	5	6	7	8	9	10
			B	L	U	E			
		W	H	I	T	E			

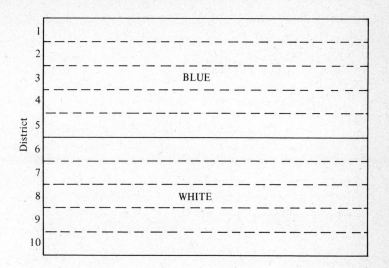

Is redistricting the guilty factor? The time periods link up very nicely—the bulk of the decline in marginal districts occurs just as redistricting is at a fever pitch. Moreover, state legislatures clearly recognize the political possibilities inherent in redistricting, as innumerable legislative stalemates and gubernatorial vetoes testify. But still, is there a reasonable doubt?

One question we might ask is, "Why the 1960s?" The states typically redistrict (or at least have the justification to redistrict) following each dicennial census. Why then would they not get rid of the marginals in the 1940s or 1950s? Why wait until the 1960s, especially given that politically tricky redistricting was probably *easier* prior to the Supreme Court decisions, which do after all rule out the most blatant attempts to gain political advantage by tinkering with district boundaries? Why the 1960s? Are we to believe that state legislators loved and protected their congressmen more in 1965 than in 1955?

Another problem arises when we consider the distributions of the *presidential* vote in the nation's congressional districts (chapter 1). If state legislatures had simply redistricted the country into more homogeneous, safe districts, then we should pick up the same kind of bimodal pattern in the presidential vote that we do in the congressional. But we don't. The distribution of the presidential vote continues to be unimodal in 1968 and 1972, although it lists well to the shy side of 50 percent Democratic under the impact of the McGovern disaster. Can districts be designed so that they are safe for one party in congressional elections but not in presidential elections? I am dubious. In my mind a reasonable doubt about the responsibility of bipartisan redistricting has been established. And the defense has not yet rested its case.

Professor John Ferejohn presents data that cut to the heart of the matter.[4] Tufte had shown that certain large states which redistricted during the mid-sixties had fewer marginal districts after the redistricting than they had prior to the redistricting. Ferejohn asks the natural question, "What happened in those states which did not redistrict during the same time period?" He constructs table 1. Evidently redistricting is innocent. The marginals were disappearing

Table 1. Decline in Percentage of Marginal Districts in Non-Southern States

1962–66	*State Redistricted*	*State Not Redistricted*
1962	51%	51%
1966	40	28
1966–70		
1966	35%	39%
1970	27	33

Key: Each cell entry represents the percentage of congressional districts that were marginal at a particular time. In 1962, for example, 51 percent of all non-southern congressional districts were marginal. By 1966 the percentage had dropped both in states which redistricted in the interim and in states which did not.

Source: John Ferejohn, "On the Decline of Competition in Congressional Elections," *American Political Science Review,* forthcoming, July 1977. Based on University of Michigan CPS Election Studies.

just as rapidly when redistricting was not taking place as when it was. In separate studies Professors Charles Bullock and Albert Cover provide additional evidence that exonerates redistricting.[5] The defense rests.

In chapter 2 I suggested that two kinds of changes were candidates for an explanation of the vanishing marginals. The first, change in the socioeconomic heterogeneity of congressional districts, we have just considered and rejected. The second involves not congressional districts, but congressmen themselves. Are incumbents more effective now than previously? If so, why?

Professor Robert Erikson has conducted research that provides statistical estimates of the "incumbency effect," the extra percentage of the vote that appears to result simply from being an incumbent, and not from party membership, region, election year, and other factors.[6] Erikson concludes that during the 1950s and early 1960s the incumbency effect was statistically present but politically unimportant. He estimates the effect as between 1 and 2 percent of the congressional vote. But, as we have seen before, something happened during the mid-1960s. Erikson's estimates for this period jump to 5 percent. The typical marginal district congressman is no longer marginal when he runs for reelection after a term in office. How can we account for this significant increase in the value of incumbency?

One possibility involves the growing pool of resources available to incumbent congressmen but not to their opponents. Congressmen have always had the visibility that accompanies victory in one or more congressional races. After all, just being a winner is testimony to having achieved some minimum threshold of visibility in the district. Moreover, once in office the congressman can advertise. The newspapers and local radio and TV cover his positions on important legislation. Awards of projects and grants within his district are channeled through his office. He may write a short column or tape a short Washington Report for the local media. He can use the congressional frank to shower his constituents with questionnaires and newsletters, letters of congratulation and condolence, pamphlets on child care and vegetable gardens, free seeds, and various other missives. Congressmen certainly use these opportunities to communicate with their districts. Moreover, they are using these opportunities at an increasing rate. Consider figure 2, which details the volume of franked mail during the period of interest.

Evidently the use of the frank has increased remarkably in recent years, far exceeding the increase in the population of congressional districts. Notice too that the trend line rockets skyward between 1963 and 1966, precisely the time when the marginals were disappearing. (For the curious I might inject parenthetically that when the data are broken down by month, one sees that October of even-numbered years is a hot time in the old Capitol Hill Post Of-

Figure 2. Franked Mail Sent out by House and Senate Members, 1954–1970

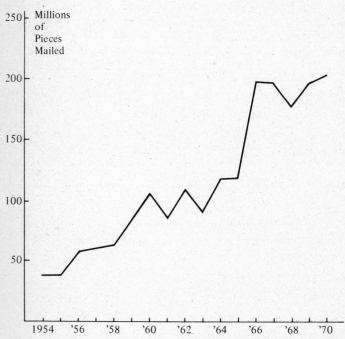

Source: Mayhew, "The Case of the Vanishing Marginals."

fice). Could the explanation for the vanishing marginals be a very simple matter of advertising? Congressmen advertise more now than they did twenty years ago and get more votes now than they did twenty years ago.

This explanation is not very complimentary to the American electorate: it suggests that citizens vote on the basis of simple name recognition. But the explanation cannot be rejected out of hand. Voting studies have typically found that "to be known at all is to be known favorably."[7] An important study carried out in 1958, for example, produced table 2.

The implications of table 2 are really rather striking. Those voters who had *no information whatsoever* on the congressional race in their district typically cast a party-line vote; about 90 percent of them did so. If the only information a voter had was about his own party's candidate, he was virtually certain to vote for that candidate. But information about the opposition party's candidate went along with a noticeable swing in support for him. In fact, those citizens who had information only about the opposition party candidate were practically an even bet to vote for him.

If we combine the preceding findings with the data on increased advertising by congressmen, we can construct the following argument. Incumbent congressmen increasingly are finding ways to contact the citizens in their districts. Such contacts produce near perfect support among members of their own party and a much

Table 2. Percentage of Party Identifiers Voting for Own Party Candidate in 1958, Contested Districts Only

Voter Aware of:	%	No. of Voters
Own candiate only	98	(166)
Neither candidate	92	(368)
Both candidates	83	(196)
Other candidates only	60	(68)

Source: Donald Stokes and Warren Miller, "Party Government and the Saliency of Congress," *Public Opinion Quarterly* 26 (1962): 631–46.

higher than expected level of support from among members of the opposition party. (Referring to the table, the argument is that incumbents are moving people out of the second category into the first and fourth categories.) As I have suggested, the argument is not very complimentary to the electorate. Can a vote really be bought by a letter of congratulation upon a high school graduation? By a district poll?

The argument has a more serious problem than whether we like it, however; other data exist that cast grave doubts upon its validity. If the argument were correct, we would expect to see the name recognition of congressional incumbents increasing over the period during which the marginals were vanishing. Do we? Consider table 3. The table reports data from academic surveys conducted under the auspices of the University of Michigan Center for Political Studies. What it shows is that incumbents are no better known following the era of the disappearing marginals than they were before it. In fact, both challengers and incumbents are perhaps a bit *less* well known. And the differential advantage of the incumbent over the challenger, if anything, has lessened between the 1950s and the 1970s. Incumbents do have an advantage over challengers in terms of name recognition, but that advantage has eroded at the same time that the incumbency advantage in congressional elections has increased.

Table 3. Voter Awareness of House Candidates in Contested Districts, 1958–1974

	Aware of Incumbent	Aware of Challenger	Comparative Advantage of Incumbent
1958	58%	38%	+20%
1964	63	40	+23
1966	56	38	+18
1968	64	47	+17
1970	55	31	+24
1974	60	44	+16

Source: Ferejohn, "On the Decline of Competition."

In sum, Common Cause, the League of Women Voters, and other "public" interest groups may deplore the existence of congressional "perks" such as the frank which seemingly give incumbents an unfair advantage. But there is no indication in the data that incumbents really profit greatly from the use of their perks, although they certainly do make use of them. We really have no choice but to release a second suspect for lack of evidence.

We are not yet out of suspects, however. Those researchers who have gathered the data that cast doubt on the explanations so far considered have put forth their own explanation for the decline of the marginals. This third explanation denies that state legislatures or public-relations-minded congressmen are behind the vanishing marginals. Rather, the voters are responsible: voters have changed the principles on which their congressional votes depend. In order to discuss this third argument I must digress briefly to present some general background on American voting behavior.

The classic voting studies carried out during the 1950s stressed the importance of party identification for a comprehensive explanation of American voting behavior.[8] The studies held that party identification is a psychological attachment to one of the two major parties. In the 1950s these identifications appeared to be very stable—people did not change their identification even when they decided to vote for the candidate of the other party. Moreover, party identification was the single best predictor of the vote, although by no means perfect. (Some Democrats did vote for Eisenhower, and 20 percent of the population did not identify with either party.) These findings about presidential voting appeared to have stark analogues on the congressional level. The evidence seemed conclusive that the congressional vote, particularly during mid-term elections, was a party-line vote.[9] In the general absence of information about the congressional candidates, most citizens simply voted for the candidate bearing the label of the party with which they identified. Turn back to table 1 in this chapter. Taking the table as a whole, 88 percent of the 789 voters included in the table voted consistently with their party identification. The decision rule for a congressional vote seemed to be a simple one: which candidate is the Democrat? (Republican)? Vote for him.

Alas, the world turns, and yesterday's truth is today's fiction. As the 1960s progressed political scientists increasingly came to see that the findings of the 1950s voting studies did not extend to all times and places.[10] The 1960s voter seemed different in several important ways from the 1950s voter. He was not so likely to have a party identification: the number of self-identified independents approximately doubled between the mid-fifties and today. Even those with a party identification were not so likely to follow it when making their voting decisions. The 1960s voter seemed to have more information about the issues and candidates and to use such information when he voted. And why not? The 1960s witnessed the rise of issues that impinged on the everyday lives of American citizens. These issues, moreover, cut across existing party alignments. A Democratic president sent the sons of the working class to die in a far away war. The urban strongholds of the Democratic party degenerated into a battleground where race fought race and criminals plundered society. Meanwhile, the adolescent children of the upper middle class gleefully seized the opportunity to overthrow moral and behavioral standards which their parents evaded but generally accepted. Facing such conditions a party identification based on the Great Depression seemed increasingly removed from the politics of the 1960s. Some disillusioned party identifiers moved into the ranks of the independents. And large numbers of the maturing baby boom, finding little that was relevant to their concerns in the existing party system, did likewise.

Posed against the stability of the 1950s was the instability of the late 1960s. A moribund Republican party came out of the grave dug in 1964 and floored the country's "majority" party in 1968. A strong third party movement arose and threatened to materially affect the outcome of the 1968 election. We heard talk of "emerging Republican majorities," the end of two-party politics, the decomposition of parties, and other grand changes.[11] Indisputably, times had changed.

In this context several researchers propounded a third explanation for the decline of the marginals, an explanation based on the behavioral changes that were occurring in the American electorate. Professors Walter Burnham, Robert Erikson, John Ferejohn, and others suggested that the intense and unstable national politics of the 1960s pushed some part of the citizenry into abandoning old principles of congressional voting, party identification in particular.[12] Advocates of this behavioral change view suggested that party identification traditionally had served as a "cue," or rule of thumb, to guide voting when the voter had little other information. So long as the parties stand for somewhat contrasting policies on issues of some concern to the voter, adherence to such cues is not a bad way to make voting decisions, particularly in obscure contests, as congressional races must seem to most people. But by the late 1960s many individuals could well have second thoughts about the rationality of employing party identification as a rule of thumb. One could very well unknowingly cast a vote for a radiclib or a neanderthal as the case might be. With everything topsy-turvy on the presidential level, could one rely on party identification any longer?

Those who advocate the behavioral change view answer the preceding question in the negative or at least argue that some significant portion of the electorate answers the question in the negative. Assume for the moment, then, that some voters abandoned their usual rule of thumb—party identification—and voted on some other basis. What other basis is there? Incumbency, perhaps? The voter might reason that if he has heard nothing about the incumbent then the latter is probably not a wild man or woman, just some ordinary, reasonably satisfactory congressman. If that is the case, why change? Let the present incumbent stay in office until he makes some misstep sufficiently serious to justify chancing the unknown evils of the challenger. In sum, advocates of the behavioral change view contend that a significant part of the electorate has substituted incumbency for party identification as a simple principle on which to base a congressional vote.

Do we accept the behavioral change view, or can we raise a reasonable doubt? Certainly the view is consistent with the broad outlines of what has happened in congressional elections. Fewer and fewer congressional votes are party-line votes, as demonstrated in table 4. From the data in table 4 we see that there has been an 8–10 percent drop in the percentage of party-line votes between the midfifties and 1970. Our earlier table 2 represented something of a high

Table 4. Percentage of Party-Line Votes in House Elections

1956	82	1966	76
1958	84	1968	74
1960	80	1970	76
1962	83	1972	74
1964	79	1974	74

Source: Robert B. Arsenau and Raymond Wolfinger, "Voting Behavior in Congressional Elections," paper delivered at the annual meeting of the American Political Science Association, New Orleans, 1973. Supplemented with University of Michigan CPS Election Studies.

point for party-line voting (1958). The shifts detailed in table 4 are not monumental, of course, but the decline of the marginals does not necessarily imply large shifts. If a congressman wins by 52 percent of the vote, then picks up an additional 5 percent in the next election, he is no longer marginal. Clearly the data in table 4 allow room for that degree of change to take place.

Still, there are questions that must be faced. The behavioral change view has an internally paradoxical quality about it. Supposedly party identification is declining in importance because voters have more information about the issues and candidates on which to base their votes. The electorate is a bit more alert and informed than it used to be. Isn't it somewhat curious that this same electorate would turn to the rather simpleminded rule of voting for incumbents? In essence, advocates of the behavioral change view would have us believe that congressional voting behavior has gotten dumber because the electorate has gotten smarter. A curious argument, I would say.

Even more serious, I think, is the existence of an abundance of data documenting the increasing alienation and cynicism of the American people. Professor Arthur Miller has analyzed much of this data.[13] He reports that between 1964 and 1970 trust in the government in Washington dropped 25 percent, beliefs that the government caters to a few big interests rose 20 percent, beliefs that the government habitually wastes money rose more than 20 percent, confidence in the competence of government officials dropped 17 percent. Even more to the point, a Harris survey found that between 1966 and 1973 confidence in the U.S. House of Representatives dropped 13 percent and in the Senate 12 percent.[14] Such data clearly show that the American citizenry is increasingly dubious about government intentions, competence, and efficiency. But advocates of the behavioral change view are aruging that these same citizens are increasingly supportive of the objects of their cynicism. The juxtaposition of these arguments casts a cloud of implausibility over the simple behavioral change view. Again, a reasonable doubt has been established.

All of the evidence discussed in this chapter has referred to elections for the U.S. House of Representatives. What of the Senate? Is the decline of the marginals purely a House phenomenon, or is a similar phenomenon apparent in Senate elections? Political scientists have examined the House much more closely than the Senate. There are 435 House elections every two years, enough to insure that idiosyncratic variation will cancel out and allow general patterns to emerge. In contrast, there are only thirty to thirty-five Senate elections every two years, and the greater visibility and media attention to the candidates and races create more variability in the results. Nevertheless, Professor Warren Kostroski has published a study which suggests that the Senate has undergone the same kind of change that is more clearly evident in the House.[15] Recall that Erikson estimated that the House incumbency effect jumped from less than 2 percent to 5 percent in the mid-sixties. Kostroski produces estimates of the independent effect of incumbency in Senate elections that show even more dramatic change. For Democratic senators Kostroski estimates an incumbency effect of 4 percent in 1948–52, increasing steadily to 12 percent in 1966–70. For Republicans the increase is from 1 percent to 11 percent over the same period. Needless to point out, senators' constituencies—states—are not subject to redistricting—one final nail in the coffin of the redistricting argument.

What do we have to show for this lengthy hunt for the people, events, or conditions that are responsible for the disappearing marginals? Nothing that is sufficient to convict, so to speak. We know that some kind of incumbency effect exists and apparently has come to exert an increasingly important influence on Congressional elections. But we cannot specify the exact nature of this effect, nor can we explain why it has grown stronger over time.

We have picked up some clues, however. We know that voters are not following their party identifications in their congressional voting as much as they used to. We know that congressmen are advertising more. We know that name recognition of the incumbent has not increased. We know that the most apparent institutional change—redistricting—can be ruled out. But what explanation is consistent with these clues? Why have the marginals disappeared? Perhaps we can find additional clues by interrogating two districts, one marginal, one ex-marginal. A study of two districts obviously cannot provide sufficient evidence for a conviction, but it might be enough to get another indictment.

Chapter 4
A Tale of Two Districts

Each of us has had the experience of searching very hard for something only to find it right under our noses. After reading and pondering the studies on which the preceding chapter is based, I began to wonder whether some analogous oversight was occurring in the search for the cause(s) of the vanishing marginals. Could there be some obvious factor that our search was overlooking, some major change that would be apparent to anyone who took a detailed look at a few selected congressional districts rather than a gross look at all districts? Believing the effort to be worth the try, I decided to do a case study of two carefully chosen congressional districts. This study involved the usual examination of the electoral returns and demographic characteristics of the districts. But in addition to these standard methods, I decided to visit the districts, to walk the same streets and travel the same roads as the congressional candidates, and to talk to some of the same people whom they talk to.

Obvious criteria guided the selection of the districts. I wanted a vanishing marginal for one of the two. How do the local observers explain the changes that have occurred between the late fifties and the present? For the second district I chose one of the few remaining marginals, a district which has easily been one of the five most competitive congressional districts in the country during the postwar period. What might distinguish this rare survivor from the district that joined the ranks of the safe ones during the 1960s?

Other considerations could not be ignored. The districts should come from the same region; it would be foolish to choose one district from the South and one from the Northeast, say, because of other differing political trends in those regions. If possible, the districts should come from within the same state. Thus voters within the districts would have been faced with the same menu of choices in both presidential and state-level elections. It would be nice if the districts had reasonably similar demographic profiles; if one had more cows than people, and the other never saw a cow uncooked, inference might be rendered difficult. Requirements like these narrowed the set of interesting districts fairly quickly.

Fortunately, I was able to locate two districts that met the criteria outlined above. After general background research on the districts, I visited each for a week to observe the local scene first hand and discuss the district's congressional politics with local party officials, newspaper reporters, ex-congressmen, defeated congressional candidates, state legislators from districts within the congressional districts, and district staff employees of the incumbent congressmen. Their views were not always mutually consistent, far from it, but they were the source of a wealth of detailed information and tantalizing hypotheses. In order to protect the anonymity of those to whom I spoke (and to allow my colleagues the fun of guessing) I will refer to the two districts simply as district A and district B.

As indicated, both districts are in the same state. Neither would be classified as metropolitan nor rural. Rather, each contains a medium-sized city and an important agricultural sector. Both districts include more than two entire counties within their boundaries. From a demographic standpoint, there is little to choose between the two districts. Their occupational, educational, and income profiles are quite similar. Neither district contains a large minority population, although there were some racial incidents in district A during the late sixties. District B has a heavier concentration of southern and eastern European immigrant stock than does district A. The religious breakdowns of the two districts are similar, however. In short, a gross look at the characteristics of the two districts does not reveal any striking differences that might correspond to the dramatic disparity in their congressional election results since the mid-sixties.

Electorally, the two districts follow very different paths. District A is the quintessential marginal district. Since its creation in 1952 the district has sent an incumbent congressman down to defeat six times, all in general elections. Each party has won the seat with at least two different candidates during this period. No congressman has ever received as much as 58 percent of the vote, and the average winning percentage is a marginal 53+ percent of the vote. The district went Democratic in the 1964 Johnson landslide, but unlike many of his colleagues around the nation this Democratic congressman did not find himself in a safe district in 1966. On the contrary, he lost. But his replacement also failed to make district A safe. In the 1974 election, the Republican candidate won the district by only 5,000 votes out of more than 120,000 cast.

District B is another story. This district was created during the mid-forties. Between its creation and the 1964 election it chose two Republican congressmen, one for the great bulk of this time. But only during the Republican landslide of 1946 (which sent the famed or notorious—depending on your point of view—80th Congress to Washington) did the district give its winning congressional candidate a comfortable send-off. Between 1948 and 1962 the average winning percentage (always Republican) was a marginal 54+. As in district A, the Democrats captured district B in the 1964 landslide. But in contrast to district A, 1964 marked the death of a marginal in district B. The Democratic congressman retained his seat in 1966, and in the elections since he has managed an average victory percentage of more than 63 percent.

Why did the Democrat who took district A in 1964 not match the feat of his counterpart in district B? And given that he did not, why has district A not experienced a triumph of incumbency on the Republican side? One explanation we can eliminate is redistricting. District A underwent no boundary change between 1952 and 1972 and then experienced a change amounting to less than 5 percent of the district's population. The boundaries of district B have not changed an iota since World War II. What then explains the electoral differences between the two districts? Let us look more closely at district A.

During the 1950s both national and state candidates had family ties to the district, ties that worked to Republican advantage in the former case and Democratic advantage in the latter. Local observers agree that a portion of the vote shifts that ended congressional careers during this period was completely beyond the control of the congressmen or their challengers. A republican congressman captured the seat immediately following the Eisenhower era. He was a conservative from the agricultural sector of the district, a somewhat crusty personality of unquestioned integrity. The picture of this congressman which emerges from my conversations is one of an officeholder who took pride in his attendance record, perceived his job as the formulation of national policy (often the obstruction of those doing the formulating), and, in general, operated rather independently of his district. In 1964 local party officials advised their candidates to dissociate themselves from the locally unpopular Goldwater candidacy. The Republican conservative refused, saying that he would not desert his friend Barry. When Lyndon Johnson improved on John Kennedy's district showing by more than 30,000 votes, the Republican congressman followed his friend Barry into enforced retirement.

But the beneficiary of the Johnson landslide did not capitalize on his opportunity. Instead, the freshman Democrat lost his seat in 1966, lost it in fact to the conservative Republican he had defeated two years previously. The Republican won several more terms, but the district remained in the ranks of the marginals. In 1974 the congressman retired. The Republicans held the seat, but only by the narrowest of margins. It came as a considerable surprise, then, when local observers assured me that the new Republican, a freshman with one year's experience, was safe, "unbeatable," that he "could hold the seat as long as he wants it." If these observers are correct (and they came from both parties), then another marginal has vanished.

How could this be? How could such a turnabout have occurred so quickly? Several explanations were offered to me. The freshman Republican has blanketed his district with communications. Both in terms of sheer volume and "effectiveness" he has greatly escalated the level of constituency contact maintained by his predecessor. Moreover, district observers believe that the freshman Republican's voting record is more closely attuned to his constituency than was that of his very conservative predecessor. The freshman voted to override a Ford veto or two, and he has supported certain federal programs which his predecessor consistently opposed. Several times I heard a remark to the effect that "he throws a few votes our (their) way now and then." Finally, the freshman Republican regularly returns to his district and travels from gathering to gathering saying:

> I'm your man in Washington. What are your problems? How can I help you?

While generally favorable to his successor, the former Republican congressman disapproves of the amount of time his successor spends in the district:

> How can he do his job in Washington when he's back here so much? People shouldn't expect a congressman to be running back home all the time.

In sum, a clear picture of district A emerges from my visit. During the 1950s this socioeconomically heterogeneous district was buffeted by broader political forces sufficiently powerful to tip the outcome of its congressional races. During the 1960s the district elected congressmen who apparently did not make all-out efforts to maximize their vote (more on the 1964 Democrat below). Now that someone is doing so, local observers and participants are betting another marginal has vanished.

What of district B? The picture of district B which emerges is that of a district ten years ahead of district A. Prior to 1964 the district was consistently but marginally Republican. The congressman who held the seat for most of this period was involved in controversial legislative battles such as Taft-Hartley and Landrum-Griffin. He suffered politically from a personal problem, according to district contacts, and possibly more importantly from a political problem: declining Republican registration within the district. At the start of his tenure in Congress his party enjoyed a comfortable registration edge within the district. But this edge had dwindled by 1964, and today the parties are dead even. Some district politicians believe that the registration shift has little significance for national elections, that it is felt mostly on the local level. But it seems prudent to bear in mind that the triumph of incumbency in district B may reflect the changing political allegiances of the district. The defeated Republican congressman, naturally enough, is partial to this view.

Still, the Democrat who barely squeaked through in 1964 improved his margin in the Republican year of 1966 (when district Republicans fully expected to win) and has rolled up margins of 40,000 votes at times since—all this with a 50–50 split in registration. District observers agree that the strength of the congressman is bipartisan; a county chairman contends that in only one instance has any other national, state, or local candidate of either party run ahead of the Democratic congressman in the district or in the relevant common subarea of it. Can a registration shift from pro-Republican to dead even explain that kind of electoral muscle, especially when Republican turnout continues to remain generally higher than Democratic? Parenthetically, the registration shift appears to be home grown and not the result of changing composition of the district. A political reporter for the major district newspaper believes that the New Deal arrived more than half a generation late in district B. The district continues to be populated by the same kind of people. Only their registration has changed. I might also remark that registration in district A has shifted very little in recent years (Republicans have a slight edge). Any changes taking place there appear to be unrelated to registration.

Back to the point. Again, in district B we find a marked behavioral difference between the pre-1964 Republican congressman and the post-1964 Democratic congressman. Strictly speaking, the location of district B does not place it in a prime "Tuesday to Thursday club" area (East Coast areas so called because of the propensity of their congressman to put in a three-day week in Washington). In practice, however, the Democratic congressman is a member in good standing. By general agreement he is a pervasive presence in the district. He has no extensive campaign organization, although he maintains close ties with the regular party organizations in the three counties. Primarily, however, the congressman relies on his own efforts, personally working the district at a feverish pace. A party chairman from a Republican area commented:

> Congressman (Democrat) comes to see people. Congressman (former Republican) didn't. The people know (Democrat). He's the first congressman to take an active interest in them.

The Democratic incumbent maintains three well-staffed offices in the district. These offices process a steady flow of constituency requests for aid in dealing with government agencies. Social security and veterans' matters are the most common kind of work handled. In this respect we find a difference between the Democratic incumbent and his principal Republican predecessor. The latter remarked:

> When I was in office I had four staff members. Now they have a regiment. That's just not necessary. It's a waste of the taxpayer's money, a frivolous expense.

The matter of the congressional staff is worthy of special notice. The retired Republican congressman in district A spontaneously brought it up. In discussing examples of the "hypocrisy" of modern Congressmen, the retiree pointed to the 1967 expansion of the congressional staff, a particularly heinous example in his view. He stated flatly:

> No congressman could possibly use sixteen staff members.

Necessity aside, the Democratic congressman in district B is using them (ten in his district), and they don't appear to be hurting him any. In fact, a principal campaign theme of this congressman has been (years before Jimmy Carter and Ronald Reagan):

> Send me to Washington. I will protect the little guy from the government.

No doubt he needs lots of staff to help him in his efforts.

Clearly, our two districts indicate that major changes in their congressional election patterns go hand in hand with behavioral changes on the part of the congressmen they elected, although the direction of causality is not yet clear. What might produce the kind of behavioral differences we observe between the pre-1964 Republican and the post-1964 Democrat in district B, and between the pre- and post-1974 Republicans in district A? The former Republican congressmen in the two districts lean toward the view that today's congressmen are of lower quality than the pre-1960 variety. Oversimplifying somewhat, in olden days strong men made up the Congress. The floor debates were something to behold. Giants walked on Capitol Hill. In those halcyon days legislators legislated. They concentrated more heavily on affairs of state than do their contemporary successors. In their motivational structure the public interest stood relatively higher and reelection relatively lower than is the case among today's congressmen.

A defeated Republican in district B, for example, remarks that in an era of $10,000 annual congressional salaries only two kinds of people were congressmen: those of independent means who did not need to be beholden to anyone and those who so loved public service they would not be beholden to anyone. He likens the lot of a 1940s congressman to that of a local school board member. There wasn't any money in it, so you only did it out of duty or love. As this congressman surveys the present scene he sees a Congress composed of 435 professional officeholders most of whom could not possibly earn $45,000 plus perks in the private sector. Perhaps he's right.

But political scientists are justifiably skeptical of theories which postulate that human nature has changed for the worse, that yesterday's political giants have given way to today's political pygmies. I will not contend that today's congressmen are more concerned with reelection than were their 1940s and 1950s predecessors. In all likelihood, since the New Deal era the average congressman's desire for reelection has remained constant. What has changed is the set of resources he possesses to invest in his reelection effort. Today's congressmen have more productive political strategies than previously. And these strategies are an unforeseen (at least by us) by-product of the growth of an activist federal government.

To elaborate, a plausible explanation of the political histories of our two cases looks rather simple. The changing nature of congressional elections in these two districts stems directly from the changing behavior of the congressmen who represented them. Both districts are heterogeneous in a socioeconomic sense and consequently in their basic political allegiances (e.g. as illustrated by registration). So long as these districts are represented by congressmen who function principally as national policymakers (pre-1964 in district B, pre-1974 in district A), reasonably close congressional elections will naturally result. For every voter a congressman pleases by a policy stand he will displease someone else. The consequence is a marginal district. But if we have incumbents who deemphasize controversial policy positions and instead place heavy emphasis on nonpartisan, nonprogrammatic constituency service (for which demand grows as government expands), the resulting blurring of political friends and enemies is sufficient to shift the district out of the marginal camp. We do not need to postulate a congressman who is more interested in reelection today than previously. All we need postulate is a congressman sufficiently interested in reelection that he would rather be reelected as an errand boy than not be reelected at all.

The critical question is whether we can expand and flesh out the preceding explanation and use it to explain the national decline in marginal districts. I think we can.

The Washington establishment now lies before us.

Distributed by Chicago Tribune-New York News Syndicate

Chapter 5
The Rise of the Washington Establishment

Dramatis Personae

In this chapter, the heart of the book, I will set out a theory of the Washington establishment(s). The theory is quite plausible from a commonsense standpoint, and it is consistent with the specialized literature of academic political science. Nevertheless, it is still a theory, not proven fact. Before plunging in let me bring out in the open the basic axiom on which the theory rests: the self-interest axiom.

I assume that most people most of the time act in their own self-interest. This is not to say that human beings seek only to amass tangible wealth but rather to say that human beings seek to achieve their own ends—tangible and intangible—rather than the ends of their fellow men. I do not condemn such behavior nor do I condone it (although I rather sympathize with Thoreau's comment that "if I knew for a certainty that a man was coming to my house with the conscious design of doing me good, I should run for my life.").[1] I only claim that political and economic theories which presume self-interested behavior will prove to be more widely applicable than those which build on more altruistic assumptions.

What does the axiom imply when used in the specific context of this book, a context peopled by congressmen, bureaucrats, and voters? I assume that the primary goal of the typical congressman is reelection. Over and above the $45,000 salary plus "perks" and outside money, the office of congressman carries with it prestige, excitement, and power. It is a seat in the cockpit of government. But in order to retain the status, excitement, and power (not to mention more tangible things) of office, the congressman must win reelection every two years. Even those congressmen genuinely concerned with good public policy must achieve reelection in order

to continue their work. Whether narrowly self-serving or more
publicly oriented, the individual congressman finds reelection to be
at least a necessary condition for the achievement of his goals.[2]

Moreover, there is a kind of natural selection process at work in
the electoral arena. On average, those congressmen who are not primarily interested in reelection will not achieve reelection as often
as those who are interested. We, the people, help to weed out congressmen whose primary motivation is not reelection. We admire
politicians who courageously adopt the aloof role of the disinterested statesman, but we vote for those politicians who follow our
wishes and do us favors.

What about the bureaucrats? A specification of their goals is
somewhat more controversial—those who speak of appointed officials as public servants obviously take a more benign view than those
who speak of them as bureaucrats. The literature provides ample
justification for asserting that most bureaucrats wish to protect and
nurture their agencies. The typical bureaucrat can be expected to
seek to expand his agency in terms of personnel, budget, and mission. One's status in Washington (again, not to mention more tangible things) is roughly proportional to the importance of the
operation one oversees. And the sheer size of the operation is taken
to be a measure of importance. As with congressmen, the specified
goals apply even to those bureaucrats who genuinely believe in their
agency's mission. If they believe in the efficacy of their programs,
they naturally wish to expand them and add new ones. All of this
requires more money and more people. The genuinely committed
bureaucrat is just as likely to seek to expand his agency as the
proverbial empire-builder.[3]

And what of the third element in the equation, us? What do we,
the voters who support the Washington system, strive for? Each of
us wishes to receive a maximum of benefits from government for
the minimum cost. This goal suggests maximum government efficiency, on the one hand, but it also suggests mutual exploitation on
the other. Each of us favors an arrangement in which our fellow
citizens pay for our benefits.

With these brief descriptions of the cast of characters in hand, let
us proceed.

Tammany Hall Goes to Washington

What should we expect from a legislative body composed of individuals whose first priority is their continued tenure in office? We should expect, first, that the normal activities of its members are those calculated to enhance their chances of reelection. And we should expect, second, that the members would devise and maintain institutional arrangements which facilitate their electoral activities. These general propositions are the focus of the remainder of this book.

For most of the twentieth century, congressmen have engaged in a mix of three kinds of activities: lawmaking, pork barreling, and casework. Congress is first and foremost a lawmaking body, at least according to constitutional theory. In every postwar session Congress "considers" thousands of bills and resolutions, many hundreds of which are brought to a record vote (over 500 in each chamber in the 93rd Congress). Naturally the critical consideration in taking a position for the record is the maximization of approval in the home district. If the district is unaffected by and unconcerned with the matter at hand, the congressman may then take into account the general welfare of the country. (This sounds cynical, but remember that "profiles in courage" are sufficiently rare that their occurrence inspires books and articles.) Abetted by political scientists of the pluralist school, politicians have propounded an ideology which maintains that the good of the country on any given issue is simply what is best for a majority of congressional districts. This ideology provides a philosophical justification for what congressmen do while acting in their own self-interest.

A second activity favored by congressmen consists of efforts to bring home the bacon to their districts. Many popular articles have been written about the pork barrel, a term originally applied to rivers and harbors legislation but now generalized to cover all manner of federal largesse.[4] Congressmen consider new dams, federal buildings, sewage treatment plants, urban renewal projects, etc. as sweet plums to be plucked. Federal projects are highly visible, their economic impact is easily detected by constituents, and sometimes they even produce something of value to the district. The average constituent may have some trouble translating his congressman's vote on some civil rights issue into a change in his personal welfare. But the workers hired and supplies purchased in connection with a big federal project provide benefits that are widely appreciated. The historical importance congressmen attach to the pork barrel is reflected in the rules of the House. That body accords certain classes of legislation "privileged" status: they may come directly to the floor without passing through the Rules Committee, a traditional graveyard for legislation. What kinds of legislation are privileged? Taxing and spending bills, for one: the government's power to raise and spend money must be kept relatively unfettered. But in addition, the omnibus rivers and harbors bills of the Public Works Committee and public lands bills from the Interior Committee share privileged status. The House will allow a civil rights or defense procurement or environmental bill to languish in the Rules Committee, but it takes special precautions to insure that nothing slows down the approval of dams and irrigation projects.

A third major activity takes up perhaps as much time as the other two combined. Traditionally, constituents appeal to their Congressman for myriad favors and services. Sometimes only information is needed, but often constituents request that their congressman intervene in the internal workings of federal agencies to affect a decision in a favorable way, to reverse an adverse decision, or simply to speed up the glacial bureaucratic process. On the basis of extensive personal interviews with congressmen, Charles Clapp writes:

> Denied a favorable ruling by the bureaucracy on a matter of direct concern to him, puzzled or irked by delays in obtaining a decision, confused by the administrative maze through which he is directed to proceed, or ignorant of whom to write, a constituent may turn to his congressman for help. These letters offer great potential for political benefit to the congressman since they affect the constituent personally. If the legislator can be of assistance, he may gain a firm ally; if he is indifferent, he may even lose votes.[5]

Actually congressmen are in an almost unique position in our system, a position shared only with high-level members of the executive branch. Congressmen possess the power to expedite and influence bureaucratic decisions. This capability flows directly from congressional control over what bureaucrats value most: higher budgets and new program authorizations. In a very real sense each congressman is a monopoly supplier of bureaucratic unsticking services for his district.

Every year the federal budget passes through the appropriations committees of Congress. Generally these committees make perfunctory cuts. But on occasion they vent displeasure on an agency and leave it bleeding all over the Capitol. The most extreme case of which I am aware came when the House committee took away the entire budget of the Division of Labor Standards in 1947 (some of the budget was restored elsewhere in the appropriations process). Deep and serious cuts are made occasionally, and the threat of such cuts keeps most agencies attentive to congressional wishes. Professors Richard Fenno and Aaron Wildavsky have provided extensive documentary and interview evidence of the great respect (and even terror) federal bureaucrats show for the House Appropriations Committee.[6] Moreover, the bureaucracy must keep coming back to Congress to have its old programs reauthorized and new ones added. Again, most such decisions are perfunctory, but exceptions are sufficiently frequent that bureaucrats do not forget the basis of their agencies' existence. For example, the Law Enforcement Assistance Administration (LEAA) and the Food Stamps Program had no easy time of it this last Congress (94th). The bureaucracy needs congressional approval in order to survive, let alone expand. Thus, when a congressman calls about some minor bureaucratic decision or regulation, the bureaucracy considers his accommodation a small price to pay for the goodwill its cooperation will produce, particularly if he has any connection to the substantive committee or the appropriations subcommittee to which it reports.

From the standpoint of capturing voters, the congressman's lawmaking activities differ in two important respects from his porkbarrel and casework activities. First, programmatic actions are inherently controversial. Unless his district is homogeneous, a congressman will find his district divided on many major issues. Thus when he casts a vote, introduces a piece of nontrivial legislation, or makes a speech with policy content he will displease some elements of his district. Some constituents may applaud the congressman's civil rights record, but others believe integration is going too fast. Some support foreign aid, while others believe it's money poured down a rathole. Some advocate economic equality, others stew over welfare cheaters. On such policy matters the congressman can expect to make friends as well as enemies. Presumably he will behave so as to maximize the excess of the former over the latter, but nevertheless a policy stand will generally make some enemies.

In contrast, the pork barrel and casework are relatively less controversial. New federal projects bring jobs, shiny new facilities, and general economic prosperity, or so people believe. Snipping ribbons at the dedication of a new post office or dam is a much more pleasant pursuit than disposing of a constitutional amendment on abortion. Republicans and Democrats, conservatives and liberals, all generally prefer a richer district to a poorer one. Of course, in recent years the river damming and stream-bed straightening activities of the Army Corps of Engineers have aroused some opposition among environmentalists. Congressmen happily reacted by absorbing the opposition and adding environmentalism to the pork barrel: water treatment plants are currently a hot congressional item.

Casework is even less controversial. Some poor, aggrieved constituent becomes enmeshed in the tentacles of an evil bureaucracy and calls upon Congressman St. George to do battle with the dragon. Again Clapp writes;

> A person who has a reasonable complaint or query is regarded as providing an opportunity rather than as adding an extra burden to an already busy office. The party affiliation of the individual even when known to be different from that of the congressman does not normally act as a deterrent to action. Some legislators have built their reputations and their majorities on a program of service to all constituents irrespective of party. Regularly, voters affiliated with the opposition in other contests lend strong support to the lawmaker whose intervention has helped them in their struggle with the bureaucracy.[7]

Even following the revelation of sexual improprieties, Wayne Hays

won his Ohio Democratic primary by a two-to-one margin. According to a *Los Angeles Times* feature story, Hays's constituency base
was built on a foundation of personal service to constituents:

> They receive help in speeding up bureaucratic action on various
> kinds of federal assistance—black lung benefits to disabled
> miners and their families, Social Security payments, veterans'
> benefits and passports.
>
> Some constituents still tell with pleasure of how Hays stormed
> clear to the seventh floor of the State Department and into
> Secretary of State Dean Rusk's office to demand, successfully,
> the quick issuance of a passport to an Ohioan.[8]

Practicing politicians will tell you that word of mouth is still the most
effective mode of communication. News of favors to constituents
gets around and no doubt is embellished in the process.

In sum, when considering the benefits of his programmatic activities, the congressman must tote up gains and losses to arrive at a
net profit. Pork barreling and casework, however, are basically
pure profit.

A second way in which programmatic activities differ from casework and the pork barrel is the difficulty of assigning responsibility
to the former as compared with the latter. No congressman can seriously claim that he is responsible for the 1964 Civil Rights Act, the
ABM, or the 1972 Revenue Sharing Act. Most constituents do have
some vague notion that their congressman is only one of hundreds
and their senator one of an even hundred. Even committee chairmen
may have a difficult time claiming credit for a piece of major legislation, let alone a rank-and-file congressman. Ah, but casework, and
the pork barrel. In dealing with the bureaucracy, the congressman
is not merely one vote of 435. Rather, he is a nonpartisan power,
someone whose phone calls snap an office to attention. He is not
kept on hold. The constituent who receives aid believes that his
congressman and his congressman alone got results. Similarly, congressmen find it easy to claim credit for federal projects awarded
their districts. The congressman may have instigated the proposal
for the project in the first place, issued regular progress reports,
and ultimately announced the award through his office. Maybe he

can't claim credit for the 1965 Voting Rights Act, but he can take credit for Littletown's spanking new sewage treatment plant.

Overall then, programmatic activities are dangerous (controversial), on the one hand, and programmatic accomplishments are difficult to claim credit for, on the other. While less exciting, casework and pork barreling are both safe and profitable. For a reelection-oriented congressman the choice is obvious.

The key to the rise of the Washington establishment (and the vanishing marginals) is the following observation: *the growth of an activist federal government has stimulated a change in the mix of congressional activities.* Specifically, a lesser proportion of congressional effort is now going into programmatic activities and a greater proportion into pork-barrel and casework activities. As a result, today's congressmen make relatively fewer enemies and relatively more friends among the people of their districts.

To elaborate, a basic fact of life in twentieth-century America is the growth of the federal role and its attendant bureaucracy. Bureaucracy is the characteristic mode of delivering public goods and services. Ceteris paribus, the more the government attempts to do for people, the more extensive a bureaucracy it creates. As the scope of government expands, more and more citizens find themselves in direct contact with the federal government. Consider the rise in such contacts upon passage of the Social Security Act, work relief projects and other New Deal programs. Consider the millions of additional citizens touched by the veterans' programs of the postwar period. Consider the untold numbers whom the Great Society and its aftermath brought face to face with the federal government. In 1930 the federal bureaucracy was small and rather distant from the everyday concerns of Americans. By 1975 it was neither small nor distant.[9]

As the years have passed, more and more citizens and groups have found themselves dealing with the federal bureaucracy. They may be seeking positive actions—eligibility for various benefits and awards of government grants. Or they may be seeking relief from the costs imposed by bureaucratic regulations—on working conditions, racial and sexual quotas, market restrictions, and numerous other subjects. While not malevolent, bureaucracies make mistakes, both of commission and omission, and normal attempts at redress often meet with unresponsiveness and inflexibility and sometimes seeming incorrigibility. Whatever the problem, the citizen's congressman is a source of succor. The greater the scope of government activity, the greater the demand for his services.

Private monopolists can regulate the demand for their product by raising or lowering the price. Congressmen have no such (legal) option. When the demand for their services rises, they have no real choice except to meet that demand—to supply more bureaucratic unsticking services—so long as they would rather be elected than un-elected. This vulnerability to escalating constituency demands is largely academic, though. I seriously doubt that congressmen resist their gradual transformation from national legislators to errand boy-ombudsmen. As we have noted, casework is all profit. Congressmen have buried proposals to relieve the casework burden by establishing a national ombudsman or Congressman Reuss's proposed Administrative Counsel of the Congress. One of the congressmen interviewed by Clapp stated:

> Before I came to Washington I used to think that it might be nice if the individual states had administrative arms here that would take care of necessary liaison between citizens and the national government. But a congressman running for reelection is interested in building fences by providing personal services. The system is set to reelect incumbents regardless of party, and incumbents wouldn't dream of giving any of this service function away to any subagency. As an elected member I feel the same way.[10]

In fact, it is probable that at least some congressmen deliberately stimulate the demand for their bureaucratic fixit services. (See the exhibit at the end of this chapter.) Recall that the new Republican in district A travels about his district saying:

> I'm your man in Washington. What are your problems? How can I help you?

And in district B, did the demand for the congressman's services rise so much between 1962 and 1964 that a "regiment" of constituency staff became necessary? Or, having access to the regiment, did the new Democrat stimulate the demand to which he would apply his regiment?

In addition to greatly increased casework, let us not forget that the growth of the federal role has also greatly expanded the federal pork barrel. The creative pork barreler need not limit himself to dams and post offices—rather old-fashioned interests. Today, creative congressmen can cadge LEAA money for the local police, urban renewal and housing money for local politicians, educational program grants for the local education bureaucracy. And there are sewage treatment plants, worker training and retraining programs, health services, and programs for the elderly. The pork barrel is full to overflowing. The conscientious congressman can stimulate applications for federal assistance (the sheer number of programs makes it difficult for local officials to stay current with the possibilities), put in a good word during consideration, and announce favorable decisions amid great fanfare.

In sum, everyday decisions by a large and growing federal bureaucracy bestow significant tangible benefits and impose significant tangible costs. Congressmen can affect these decisions. Ergo, the more decisions the bureaucracy has the opportunity to make, the more opportunities there are for the congressman to build up credits.

The nature of the Washington system is now quite clear. Congressmen (typically the majority Democrats) earn electoral credits by establishing various federal programs (the minority Republicans typically earn credits by fighting the good fight). The legislation is drafted in very general terms, so some agency, existing or newly established, must translate a vague policy mandate into a functioning program, a process that necessitates the promulgation of numerous rules and regulations and, incidentally, the trampling of numerous toes. At the next stage, aggrieved and/or hopeful constituents petition their congressman to intervene in the complex (or at least obscure) decision processes of the bureaucracy. The cycle closes when the congressman lends a sympathetic ear, piously denounces the evils of bureaucracy, intervenes in the latter's decisions, and rides a grateful electorate to ever more impressive electoral showings. Congressmen take credit coming and going. They are the alpha and the omega.

The popular frustration with the permanent government in Washington is partly justified, but to a considerable degree it is misplaced resentment. *Congress is the linchpin of the Washington establishment.* The bureaucracy serves as a convenient lightning rod for public frustration and a convenient whipping boy for congressmen. But so long as the bureaucracy accommodates congressmen, the latter will oblige with ever larger budgets and grants of authority. Congress does not just react to big government—it creates it. All of Washington prospers. More and more bureaucrats promulgate more and more regulations and dispense more and more money. Fewer and fewer congressmen suffer electoral defeat. Elements of the electorate benefit from government programs, and all of the electorate is eligible for ombudsman services. But the general, long-term welfare of the United States is no more than an incidental by-product of the system.

Exhibit: How the Congressman-as-Ombudsman Drums up Business

NEED HELP WITH A FEDERAL PROBLEM?

Please feel free to communicate with me, in person, by phone or by mail. Daily from 9 a.m. until 5 p.m. my Congressional District office in Fullerton is open to serve you and your family. The staff will be able to help you with information or assistance on proposed Federal legislation and procedures of Federal agencies. If you are experiencing a problem with Social Security, educational assistance, Veterans Administration, Immigration, Internal Revenue Service, Postal Service, Environmental Protection Agency, Federal Energy Office or any other Federal agency, please contact me through this office. If you decide to write to me, please provide a telephone number as many times I can call you with information within a day or two.

CONGRESSMAN CHARLES E. WIGGINS
Brashears Center, Suite 103
1400 N. Harbor Boulevard
Fullerton, Ca 92635 (714) 870-7266

My Washington address is
Room 2445 Rayburn Building, Washington, D.C.
20515. Telephone (202) 225-4111.

U.S. House of Representatives
WASHINGTON, D.C. 20515
PUBLIC DOCUMENT
OFFICIAL BUSINESS

Charles E. Wiggins
M.C.

POSTAL CUSTOMER-LOCAL
39th District
CALIFORNIA

Chapter 6
Back to the Vanishing Marginals: Some Loose Ends

As I suggested in the previous chapter, the marginals disappeared as the Washington system developed. Congressmen elected from marginal districts found it increasingly possible to base their reelection on their noncontroversial activities—their casework and success in procuring the pork—rather than on their lawmaking activities, which divided their districts. As Congress created a government ever larger and more far-reaching, it simultaneously increased the opportunities for its members to build up political credit with their constituents. In effect, I am proposing a behavioral change theory. Burnham, Erikson, and Ferejohn are correct: voting behavior in congressional elections has changed. But I think that the explanations of these authors are incomplete. Voting behavior did not change by itself. Rather, voting behavior changed in part because congressional behavior changed. Congressmen are not simply passive reactors to a changing electoral climate. They have helped to change that climate.

Several subsidiary questions still remain without satisfactory answers, however. In this short chapter I would like to address three of them. First, what is the exact nature of the congressional incumbency effect? Second, are the hypothesized changes in congressional behavior sufficiently large to account for the vanishing marginals? Third, what about the timing of the electoral shift, its abrupt nature?

The Nature of the Incumbency Effect

If an increasing number of congressmen are devoting increasing resources to constituency service, then we would expect that increasing numbers of voters must think of their congressmen less as policymakers than as ombudsmen and pork barrelers. If so, other implications are immediate. First, party identification will be less influential in determining the congressional vote, not just because of the unusual national politics of the late 1960s, but because *objectively* the congressman is no longer as policy relevant as he once was. In legislative matters he is merely one vote of 435. But in bureaucratic matters he is a benevolent, nonpartisan power. And if more and more citizens come to think of their congressmen in this manner, then the basis of the incumbency effect is obvious. *Experience in Washington and congressional seniority count when dealing with the bureaucracy.* So long as the incumbent can elude a personal morality rap and refrain from casting outlandish votes, he is naturally preferred over a newcomer. *This incumbency effect is not only understandable; it is rational.* And it would grow over time as increasing numbers of citizens come to regard their congressman as a troubleshooter in the Washington bureaucracies.

Recall the troublesome table 3 from Chapter 3. Some draw the seemingly reasonable conclusion that the incumbency effect is unrelated to the communications incumbents shower on their constituents, because the informational advantage incumbents possess did not increase between 1958 and 1974, while the incumbency advantage apparently increased during this period. But what if the *content* of the information has changed over time? What if in 1958 those voters who had heard or read something about the incumbent had heard or read about one or more of his policy stands, whereas in 1970 they had heard or read about his effectiveness in getting Vietnam veterans' checks in the mail? Some voters will agree with the policy stand, others will disagree, but everyone will applaud efforts in behalf of the veterans. Even if the proportion aware of the incumbent has stayed constant around 50 percent, one would expect him to capture a larger chunk of that 50 percent if his constituents' knowledge relates to his casework and pork-barrel activities rather than to his policy positions. Thus an increasing incumbency advantage is quite consistent with a constant informational advantage if information about the incumbent has grown increasingly noncontroversial in content and correspondingly positive in its impact.

Furthermore, as suggested above, if popular perceptions of the congressman gradually change from national legislator to district ombudsman, even those citizens having no specific information about incumbent or challenger act quite sensibly in going with the candidate who has experience and seniority.

Thus there are good reasons to anticipate an incumbency effect both among those with specific political information about the incumbent and among those without such information. Moreover, that effect is not an irrational response to a familiar name; rather, it is a justifiable response to a changed political reality.

The Magnitude of the Incumbency Effect

Some of my colleagues have conceded that the trends I have hypo-thesized probably are occurring but have expressed doubt that the magnitude of the behavioral changes could account for the decline of the marginals. A congressman would have to do one hell of a lot of personal favors, they say. And congressmen still seem to spend some time passing laws.

For clarity's sake I have presented my arguments in bold outline. But in order to account for the decline of the marginals we do *not* need to claim that *all* congressmen have opted exclusively for an ombudsman role and that *all* constituents now think of their con-gressman in nonprogrammatic terms. In actuality, the disappearance of a marginal requires only marginal (no pun intended) change. To illustrate, let us take Mayhew's bimodal vote distribution for 1972 and take away Erikson's estimated 5 percent incumbency effect. That is, we assume that no incumbency effect exists, so 5 percent is subtracted from the vote of each incumbent running in 1972. Figures 3a and 3b compare the 1972 vote distribution with the hypothetical deflated one.

The large difference between the distributions even surprised me when I performed the calculations. Just taking away a 5 percent incumbency effect wipes out the trough in the middle range of the actual vote distribution. Subtracting a hypothetical *10 percent* effect returns the distribution to the 1948 appearance. The con-clusion seems obvious. To explain the vanishing marginals we need

Figure 3a. Congressional Vote in Districts with Incumbents Running, 1972

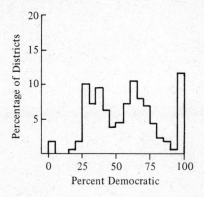

Figure 3b. Congressional Vote in Districts with Incumbents Running Minus 5 Percent Incumbency Advantage, 1972

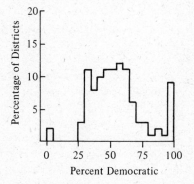

only argue that over the past quarter of a century expanded constituency service and pork-barrel opportunities have given the marginal congressman the opportunity to switch 3-5 percent of those who would otherwise oppose him on policy grounds to his supporting coalition. Considering the magnitude of the growth in the federal role during that same period, such a shift seems eminently plausible.

The Timing of the Changes

The growth of the federal role has been reasonably continuous albeit with definite take-off points such as tne New Deal and World War II. The decline of congressional competition, in contrast, has been somewhat more erratic. No change was noticeable before the 1950s, and the most pronounced change appears to have occurred over a relatively short period during the mid-sixties. How do we reconcile the differences in the two trends?

One would expect some lag between the onset of bureaucratic expansion and the decline of the marginals, because congressmen presumably would not grasp the new opportunities immediately. Moreover, the effects of federal expansion are cumulative. In the early part of the postwar period congressmen may have used their opportunities to the fullest, but the electoral impact might have been imperceptible. By the 1960s however, constituency service opportunities had cumulated to a significant electoral factor.

Still, the mid-sixties decline is especially pronounced. I think it is probably too much to argue that Great Society programs translated into casework and then votes quite so immediately. But one possible explanation of the sixties decline lies in recent work by Professor Richard Fenno.[1] Fenno attaches great importance to a congressman's "homestyle," his basic patterns of interaction with his district. Homestyle includes three components: (1) the congressman's allocation of time, effort, and staff to his district, (2) his personal style, and (3) his explanation for his Washington activities. Most relevant for my discussion are Fenno's observations about the constraints imposed by homestyles. Fenno argues that congressional careers pass through two stages, expansionist and protectionist, and

> Once in the protectionist phase . . . the dominant impulse is conservative. Keep the support you had "last time"; do what you did "last time." The tendency to follow established patterns, to observe stylistic constraints, is strong.[2]

Now when one considers that between the 88th and 90th Congresses (1963-67) one-third of the membership of the House changed, a plausible hypothesis emerges. The new representatives placed relatively greater emphasis on constituency service than did those whom they replaced. The average freshman in 1965 replaced a congressman elected in 1952 or 1954. The latter had formed their homestyles in a different era. Moreover, particularly in 1964 many of the freshmen were Democrats who had won election in heretofore Republican districts. They can hardly be blamed for assuming that they could not win reelection on policy grounds. They had every incentive to adopt homestyles that emphasized nonprogrammatic constituency service. (And, I might add, if they were not smart enough to see that themselves, it was pointed out to them. The congressional party leadership assisted by the American Political Science Association, emphasized the importance of constituency service during the 1964 orientation sessions!) I might also point out that the Democrat who won district A in 1964 and lost it in 1966 did not follow the good advice offered him. According to local supporters, he was seldom heard from, even during the 1966 campaign. He became totally engrossed in his Washington affairs.

Paradoxically, then, the electoral upheavals of the 1960s may have produced the electoral stability of the early 1970s. New congressmen chose homestyles best adapted to the changed congressional environment. Is it purely coincidence that these fresh Congresses have raised personal staff allotments by over 50 percent since 1967? (More on this in chapter 7).

Chapter 7
Some Circumstantial Evidence
Surrounding the Rise of the
Washington Establishment

In an earlier chapter (5) I discussed the kinds of activities favored by congressmen oriented toward reelection and how the mix of those activities has changed as the federal government has grown. The discussion was relatively theoretical. Congressmen, after all, do not keep public records of the time they spend in various activities. In this chapter I will discuss several ways in which congressmen have altered their institutional surroundings in order to facilitate the performance of electorally profitable activities. In this area more evidence is available, although it is of a circumstantial nature. It takes on significance when examined in light of the previously developed argument.

During the past twenty years, congressional incumbents have adopted various plans to increase the resources available for investment in their reelection efforts and to modify existing institutional arrangements to better serve their electoral ends. One highly visible change is the doubling of their personal staffs. A second is the continual increase in various congressional "perks." A third, more far-reaching change, is the devolution of congressional power from full committee to subcommittee level, thereby giving rank-and-file congressmen a bigger piece of the action and producing a proliferation of "subgovernments" in Washington. Finally, I will discuss the creation of formal legislative liaison offices in the bureaucracy, an executive innovation which incumbent congressmen have used to good advantage.

The Congressional Staff

Sad to say, the subject of the congressional staff is largely a neglected one. The few published studies by political scientists deal with committee staffs, the professional and clerical employees of the standing committees. My concern is with the personal staffs of congressmen, something of a lively topic at the time of this writing (although Miss Ray was a committee staff employee). Recall from chapter 4 how a defeated congressman complained that compared to his former staff the present Democratic incumbent had a "regiment." The former congressman's observation is a legitimate one. Office staff authorizations are stated in terms of both a maximum number of employees and a maximum base payroll. The story of both in the past twenty years has been quite simple: steady expansion.

In the early 1960s, before the disappearance of the marginals became apparent, each member of the House was authorized to hire up to nine staff at a basic total payroll of some $20,000, a number in practice augmented to about $50,000 by numerous pay raise enactments. During the 1960s the authorization crept up to eleven, then to fifteen by 1971 at a total payroll of more than $141,000. (Members who had heavily populated districts—over 500,000—were allowed one extra employee during this period.) Today congressmen are allowed up to eighteen staff on a total payroll of more than $225,000. Thus we have seen a doubling of personal staff resources during the past fifteen years, most of which occurred at the same time the marginal districts were disappearing. In the Senate, staff sizes are tied to state population, but there too the story is the same: rapid expansion. Currently senators receive between $400,000 and $800,000 annually to hire personal staff, plus an extra $100,000 for three staff earmarked to aid with committee work.

Table 5 details some features of the congressional staff at three points in time: prior to the decline of the marginals and the staff expansions of the 1960s, while both were occurring, and following the decline in the marginals and the doubling of the staffs. The simple increase in the number of authorized staff is clearly apparent, from 2,300 in 1960 to more than 5,000 in 1974. Rather more interesting are the other three pieces of data. First, the percent of staff assigned to the home districts has more than doubled, from 14 percent of all listed staff members in 1960 to 34 percent in 1974. Second, congressional staff operations in the district are now permanent operations.

Table 5. Growth of Personal Staffs of Congressmen, 1960–1974

	1960	*1967*	*1974*
Total staff	2,344	3,276	5,109
Percentage of total staff assigned to district offices	14%	26%	34%
Percentage of congressmen whose district offices open only when congressman is home or after adjournment	29%	11%	2%
Percentage of congressmen listing multiple district offices	4%	18%	47%

Source: Annual Congressional Staff Directories, compiled by Charles B. Brownson.

In 1960 nearly 30 percent of all congressmen specified that their district offices were open only when they were home or after the adjournment of Congress. Today one can find only slight traces of intermittent staff operations.[1] Third, district staff offices as well as district staff have increased. In 1960 only 4 percent of all congressmen listed more than one district office (generally two; only one congressman listed three). But by the mid-seventies we see that multiple offices are the case as often as not.

What are the duties of these growing numbers of congressional staff? Unfortunately, the little data available are both extremely fragmentary and rather dated. The occasional academic writings on the subject tend to rely on the same sketchy figures, so I have little choice but to do likewise. A mid-sixties survey of congressional staffs produced the data summarized in table 6.

If these data are representative, then members of the House spend nearly 30 percent of their time on constituency service, while their staffs spend well over half their time on such matters. (Bear in mind too that some legislative matters are directly constituency related—authorization of various district projects, for example.) If anything, the data may understate the constituency service function. Congres-

Table 6. Average Washington Work Week of Congressman and Personal Staff

Function	Congressman	Personal Staff
Legislative	65%	14%
Constituency service	28	25
Education/publicity	8	10
Correspondence (mix of constituency service and education)	–	41
Other	–	10

Source: Adapted from John Saloma, Congress and the New Politics (Boston: Little, Brown, 1969), Tables 6.5 and 6.7, pp. 184–85. Data on congressional work week based on returns from 150 offices, on staff work week from 60 offices.

sional scholar Kenneth Olson, who has studied the casework load, estimates that

> the chances are good that an analysis of the total time expended by members and their staffs on all congressional work would find casework the leading activity.[2]

Moreover, the data in the table should be read in the light of two additional considerations. First, the casework load no doubt has increased since the data were gathered in 1965. Even if congressmen did not consciously try to expand the casework burden, the increase in federal programs over the last ten years surely has stimulated a large number of additional requests. Second, the data in table 6 refer to the work week of the *Washington* office. Presumably the *district* offices are totally absorbed in constituency service. Thus the expansion in the district staff operations documented in table 5 represents almost entirely increases in constituency services.

There is an ironic twist to the story of the congressional staff expansions. Of all the possible changes ("reforms") that various observers have urged upon Congress during the postwar period, staff increases are perhaps the least controversial. Congressional actions to augment staff numbers and quality are almost universally encouraged and applauded. The reason is a naïve assumption about the purposes to which congressmen put their staffs. Reformers correctly see that the world has grown much more complex in recent years, that policy matters now require more than the commonsense of the "man from Missouri." Economic, technological, and social scientific expertise is critically important for making effective public policy decisions. The executive is well endowed with such expertise, but for years congressmen plodded along with a clerk and a secretary. To reformers, a large professional staff is just the thing to assure better public policies and a more even balance between Congress and the executive branch.

But in reality what are the uses to which congressmen put their staffs? Improved public policy is a goal that most congressmen favor. But reelection is certainly a more important goal. And when given sixteen or eighteen employees to allocate as they see fit, congressmen quite naturally put the lion's share to work on the most important thing, reelection, while perhaps reserving a few for secondary matters such as formulating our country's laws and programs.

Other Perquisites of Office

When public interest groups criticize the advantages of incumbency, they generally are referring to a variety of tangible resources freely available to incumbents but not to their challengers. In addition to the well-known congressional frank, congressmen receive allowances for postage (airmail and special delivery), stationery and office supplies, telephone and telegraph use, and travel to their home districts. When we look at any of these allowances over the period of our study, the story is the expected one: they go up.[3]

Naturally we expect some increase in the various allowances. Inflation has steadily pushed up the price of stationery, air fares, and office rental. And, of course, postal rates have increased. But Congress has more than kept up with inflation. The 1965 increase in office rental allowances, for example, also included authorization for more district offices. The increases documented in row four of table 5 reflect more than just keeping up with inflation.

The case of travel allowances is no doubt the most interesting. In the early 1960s, before the noticeable drop in the number of marginal districts, members of the House and Senate were authorized to make three expense-paid round trips home each year. By 1966 the Senate had increased the authorization to six per year, while the House had upped it to five. By 1968 congressmen were allowed one trip for each month the Congress was in session, for a maximum of twelve per year, while senators were authorized a flat twelve per year. By 1973 representatives were up to eighteen trips per year. At present congressmen are entitled to twenty-six trips home per year, while senators receive forty-two to forty-six. (House and Senate *staff* also have received increasing authorization for trips to the district or state.)

Congressmen are going home more, pressing the flesh, getting around. They are building a personal base of support, one dependent on personal contacts and favors. The greatly increased presence of the congressman in his district dovetails nicely with the greatly enlarged district staff operations. The travel increases also suggest a tentative answer to a question some might raise about the staff increases. To wit, are congressmen just as devoted to lawmaking activities now as ever? Have they increased the staff in order to relieve themselves of the casework burden? I don't think so.

First, the enlarged staff requires supervision; it doesn't run itself. Second, even if a constant proportion of the increased casework was "bucked" up to the congressman for his personal attention now as previously, this would still be a major increase in casework requiring his personal intervention. And, most importantly, in the two districts which I have examined closely increased attention to casework and constituency problems generally goes hand in hand with frequent presence in the district:

> How can he do his job in Washington when he's back here so much? People shouldn't expect a congressman to be running back home all the time.

The greatly increased congressional travel allowances suggest that my two cases are not exceptions. In all likelihood, both the staff and the congressman are devoting a greater proportion of their time to constituency service now than they were in the early 1960s.

In the aftermath of the Wayne Hays imbroglio the House of Representatives has taken some action to "reform" the use of special allowances. No longer are congressmen permitted to withdraw stationery or postal allowances in cash, for example. And reporting requirements have been tightened. But the reforms contain a sweetener for incumbents as well. No longer are the allowances kept separate. Now members of the House have one general fund which they can allocate as they see fit; telephone money can be used for travel, etc. They've given themselves a bit more flexibility.

In 1964, prior to the occurrence of much that has just been described, Representative Michael Kirwan (D., Ohio) wrote candidly:

> No congressman who gets elected and who minds his business should ever be beaten. Everything is there for him to use if he'll only keep his nose to the grindstone and use what is offered.[4]

The changes that have occurred since the time of Kirwan's comment only reinforce its basic accuracy.

The Continued Decentralization of Congressional Power

In chapter 1, I remarked that curbs on the arbitrary powers of the congressional party leadership at the beginning of this century were a natural outgrowth of the increasing professionalization of congressmen. With more and more congressmen wishing to retain their seats for long periods, iron party discipline became intolerable. The individual congressman desired the flexibility to follow the wishes of his district when party–district conflicts arose. Moreover, taking power from the hands of the party leadership and spreading it more widely around the chamber gave individual members a greater opportunity to take actions to enhance their reelection efforts. The seniority system was the natural response to a group of budding career congressmen. Power was distributed more widely to a larger group of standing committee chairmen (there were about sixty standing committees in 1910), who would attain their positions by the automatic workings of the seniority system. Acceptance of the seniority system gave local districts the upper hand over the national parties in the U.S. Congress.

The distribution of power within Congress remained relatively constant throughout the mid-century period, but in recent years the trend toward further decentralization rapidly picked up speed. The development of the congressional subcommittee system is the most obvious indicator.

In 1946 the Legislative Reorganization Act rationalized an overgrown, outdated full committee structure. On the face of it, the reorganization (cutting by more than half the number of standing committees) was a major centralization of formal authority. But the proliferation of subcommittees soon began to offset the major thrust of the reorganization. Since 1946 the number of full committees has increased by only one in the House and three in the Senate, but table 7 details the steady growth of subcommittees. Bear in mind that in 1973 243 majority Democrats sat in the House, while 59 sat in the Senate. On average, one of every two Democrats in the House was chairman of a subcommittee, while every Senate Democrat chaired an average of two subcommittees.

Not only has the number of subcommittees undergone a dramatic

Table 7. Growth of Congressional Subcommittee System

Year	House	Senate
1955	83	79
1963	113	90
1973	125	128

Key: Table entries are number of subcommittees of congressional standing committees.

Source: Adapted from table 5 of Norman Ornstein and David Rohde, "Seniority and Future Power in Congress," in Norman Ornstein, ed., Change in Congress (New York: Praeger, 1975), pp. 72-87.

increase, but their powers and autonomy also have increased in the wake of changes (called "reforms," of course) that occurred in the House in the early 1970s.[5] First, in 1971 members were limited to the chairmanship of one subcommittee. Senior members who were hoarding chairmanships were forced to relinquish them to less senior members. Later, in 1973, a subcommittee "bill of rights" further reinforced the devolution of power. No longer could full committee chairmen arbitrarily designate subcommittee chairmen; full committee or subcommittee seniority (depending on the wishes of the committee Democrats) would henceforth determine subcommittee chairmanships. Subcommittee jurisdictions were fixed; full committee chairmen no longer could establish vague subcommittee jurisdictions in order to maximize their own flexibility in assigning legislation. Subcommittees were guaranteed adequate budgets and staffing; no longer could a full committee chairman starve a subcommittee or pack its staff with his minions. The full impact of these changes has yet to be determined, but it is clear that twenty-odd full committee chairmen have been weakened and 120-odd subcommittee chairmen strenghtened. Congress now has a surfeit of chiefs and a shortage of Indians.

But aren't such reforms democratic (small d), one might ask? And isn't democracy good in itself? Perhaps, but democracy has its cost. In particular, those who applaud internal democratic reforms should not criticize Congress for inefficiency, shortsightedness, and foot-dragging. For example, public interest groups applaud the democratization of Congress, on the one hand, and deplore Congress' failure to formulate a national energy policy, on the other. There is something of an inconsistency here. How many are aware that in 1976 eleven subcommittees from six standing committees had a legitimate claim to a piece of the action in the energy area? These were:

1. Conservation, Energy and National Resources, chaired by Moorhead of Pennsylvania (Government Operations)
2. Water and Power Resources, chaired by Johnson of California
3. Energy and the Environment, chaired by Udall of Arizona
4. Mines and Mining, chaired by Mink of Hawaii

⎱ All of Interior and Insular Affairs

5. Energy and Power, chaired by Dingell of Michigan } Both of Interstate and Foreign Commerce

6. Health and the Environment, chaired by Rogers of Florida

7. Fisheries and Wildlife Conservation and the Environment, chaired by Leggett of California (Merchant Marines and Fisheries)

8. Water Resources, chaired by Roberts of Texas (Public Works)

9. Energy Research, Development and Demonstration, (Fossil Fuels) chaired by Hechler of West Virginia } All of Science and Technology

10. Energy Research, Development and Demonstration, chaired by McCormack of Washington

11. Environment and the Atmosphere, chaired by Brown of California

(Additionally, various Appropriations subcommittees get their thumb in the pie at that stage of the process.)

Each of these subcommittees can lay claim to some piece of any energy-environment policy decision. And given the political incentive to claim credit, most of them will do so. Moreover, compound the above division of responsibility by adding the equally elaborate one that exists in the Senate. The result is more than twenty congressional power bases for senators to advertise presidential hopes, congressmen to advertise senatorial hopes, and/or everyone to advertise reelection hopes. This is democracy in action?

Political scientists and political observers foreshadowed the rise of the Washington establishment when they wrote of "subgovernments" (journalist Douglas Cater's term), "whirlpools" (Professor Ernest Griffith's term), and "policy systems" (Professors Eugene Eidenberg's and Roy Morey's term).[6] Professor Randall Ripley writes:

> Most of the interaction between Congress and the bureaucracy represents the ongoing activities of subgovernments. The basic institutional units in typical interaction are standing subcommittees (occasionally a full committee) from the House or Senate and various administrative units below the departmental level in the executive branch such as bureaus, agencies, services, and

administrations. Much of the detailed business of the government is carried on between these units, sometimes with the participation of interest group representatives. Larger units (for example, the entire House or Senate, the White House, or the office of a departmental secretary) get involved in details much less frequently. In general, only highly visible and politically sensitive issues are likely to receive attention from the larger units; relatively less visible matters are often handled completely by a bureau speaking for the entire executive branch and a subcommittee speaking for the entire House and Senate. Individual members of the House and Senate and their staff members also get involved with the bureaucracy, usually because of a pending "case" involving a constituent.[7]

In other words, political observers are aware that cozy little groups of congressmen, bureaucrats, and interest group representatives make numerous day-to-day policy decisions. What has been less obvious is the manner in which the number of these subgovernments has been proliferating as the power of the twenty-odd full committees has been dispersed among the 120-odd subcommittees. If they so desire, most congressmen now have the opportunity to head up a subgovernment. By protecting a few agencies under their jurisdiction and accommodating a few concerned interest groups, the congressman buys electoral credit from the latter and wields influence over the former.

Two other facts of congressional life reinforce the usefulness (from the standpoint of individual congressmen) of this system of divided-up government. First, most congressmen gravitate to those committees which enable them to satisfy their reelection goal.[8] Oversimplifying, Westerners head for Interior, rural congressmen for Agriculture, inner city congressmen for Judiciary, etc. (The few generalized power committees—Appropriations, Ways and Means, Rules—stand astride the legislative process at so many points that their members can trade influence with members of all the standing committees.) Thus congressmen eventually gain influence in those subgovernments of particular concern to them and, by implication, their districts. Their power in the subgovernment translates directly into electoral credit for favorable policy decisions and successful intervention in the bureaucracy.

A second, related fact is congressional observance of reciprocity: "you scratch my back, and I'll scratch yours," or "keep your nose out of my business, and I'll reciprocate." Given that most congressmen end up in the subgovernments of particular concern to them, observance of reciprocity is not very costly in terms of lost opportunities, and it is very profitable in terms of unfettered influence in an area vital to their continued reelection.

In sum, the decentralization of congressional power has created numerous subgovernments that enable individual members to control policy decisions and influence elements of the bureaucracy which are of particular concern to their districts. Increased electoral security is the natural result. On the face of it, the system is highly democratic. But do numerous piecemeal, uncoordinated decisions motivated primarily by congressional desire for reelection add up to good public policy? Advocates of ever more democracy might well consider this question.

The Growth of Legislative Liaison

American reformers show a great fondness for tinkering with the formal rules and procedures of the political system. Too often they naïvely assume that a simple rules change will solve a problem or alleviate an undesirable situation. Too seldom do they attempt an in-depth analysis of why the problem exists. Who profits from the existing state of affairs? Who stands to lose by changes in the status quo? As a result of incomplete analyses, procedural reforms often turn out to have unanticipated consequences. Regulatory commissions protect the regulated and exploit the public. Campaign spending limits work against congressional challengers. Opening up the primary process comes uncomfortably close to giving us Hubert Humphrey in a brokered convention. And congressional staff increases make incumbents ever more secure.

In this section I wish to suggest how congressman have taken advantage of an executive innovation, an innovation probably intended to take advantage of them. The institutional innovation to which I refer is the establishment of formal legislative liaison offices within the cabinet departments of the national government. The Defense

Table 8. Growth of Legislative Liaison Personnel, Department of Defense

	1963	1965
Office of the Secretary	13	34
Army	48	92
Air Force	119	144
Navy	50	70
Total	230	340

Source: G. Russell Pipe, "Congressional Liaison: The Executive Branch Consolidates Its Relations with Congress," *Public Administration Review* 26 (1966): 14-24.

and State departments established such offices in the late 1940s. The Post Office, Commerce, and HEW followed by 1955. In the early years of the Kennedy administration, under the direction of Larry O'Brien, the establishment of liaison offices was completed.[9] Existing liaison offices also were expanded. Again, data are fragmentary, but the data in table 8 on the expansion of the Defense Liaison Office are suggestive of the mid-sixties growth.

Prior to the creation of formal offices of legislative liaison, relations between Congress and the bureaucracy took place primarily at the bureau level. Congressmen had to develop their own personal contacts on the basis of interactions in the policymaking and appropriations processes. But with the establishment of formal liaison operations (centered in the office of the cabinet secretary) congressmen gained a direct line from the top into the bureaucracy.

In theory the establishment of liaison offices would help the executive branch to lead Congress, to coordinate the decentralized power centers in that body, to show parochial committee barons why they should not amend a presidential initiative umpteen ways to Sunday. In practice, however, liaison officers are a hot line into their respective departments. A small favor for a congressman's constituent? Sure, it's a cheap price to pay for his goodwill on a legislative proposal dear to the department's heart. Washington attorney and writer

Edward de Grazia recognizes and approves of this turn of affairs:

> liaison with key members of the executive branch appears to give
> the congressman (1) direct access to those who make executive
> policy—high-ranking officials in the secretaries' offices; (2) a
> "point of view" concerning departmental administration; (3) in-
> formation about policy questions, to fill what sometimes seems
> "a vacuum"; and (4) *perhaps most importantly, assistance in the
> meeting of constituent needs.* (My emphasis)[10]

What kinds of assistance do the liaison offices provide congressmen?
De Grazia offers the example of the Agency for International Development:

> A sampling which represented probably 75 percent of the total,
> was made of matters handled in the AID Congressional Liaison
> Office during a single week. The sampling revealed 168 telephone
> calls from members of Congress and their staffs on such matters
> as: a company in Wisconsin wanting to bid on planes; a constitu-
> ent wanting an appointment on a project in Guatemala; a com-
> pany in North Dakota wanting a contract; a firm protesting an
> AID contract award to an Oregon firm; another inquiry on be-
> half of the Oregon firm; the faculty at Roberts College in Turkey
> complaining about AID clearance requirements; the population
> problem; Vietnam; housing guaranties; an OAS conference; aid
> to Yugoslavia; AID-financed procurements in the United States;
> balance of payments and gold flow; Cooley loans; and employ-
> ment interest of constituents. During that week there were also
> 84 requests from members of Congress for information; the appro-
> priate materials were assembled and sent out by the Congressional
> Liaison staff. Calls or visits were made by the staff to 71 senators
> and congressmen for the purpose of assisting them, at their re-
> quest, with various AID questions and problems. Approximately
> 75 letters were sent during that week to members of Congress in
> response to mail or telephone requests.[11]

And certainly it is doubtful that AID interests congressmen nearly
as much as HEW, HUD, the Department of Agriculture, the Social
Security Administration, or the Veterans Administration.

A fine example of congressional ingenuity comes from a short case study by Professor Randall Ripley of the congressional battle over the debt limit in 1963. Writes Ripley:

> On Friday, May 10, McCormack, Albert, John Moss (the deputy whip), and Mills met Lawrence O'Brien, chief of White House congressional liaison, three O'Brien assistants, the administrative assistant to the whip, and the Assistant Secretary of the Treasury for congressional liaison. Mills reviewed a list of all Democrats and announced their reported position on the bill. When a member was announced as doubtful or against the bill, the Speaker or Majority Leader called him immediately and urged him to support it. Likewise, when a member favoring the bill was reported as planning to be absent, the Speaker called him and asked him to stay. One member who was asked to cancel a trip abroad (which he did) *used the occasion to arrange an appointment with O'Brien for himself and another Democrat to talk about a proposed veterans hospital consolidation in their districts.* (My emphasis)[12]

Here is a neat instance of the Washington system in operation. Congressmen agree to go along with some executive desire if the price is right, the executive branch gets the support it needs, constituents see evidence of the power of their congressmen, and the latter increase their margins at the polls. Was the increase in the debt limit good policy? Who knows? Who cares?

Chapter 8
Alternative Views

In discussing the concept of a Washington establishment two distinct types of questions arise. First, does one exist, and, if so, what exactly is it? Second, is the system undesirable, and should it be changed? I have argued in the preceding pages that there is an identifiable Washington system, composed of Congress and the federal bureaucracies operating in a seemingly antagonistic but fundamentally symbiotic relationship. To recount briefly, by working to establish various federal programs (or in some cases fighting their establishment) congressmen earn electoral credit from concerned elements of their districts. Some federal agency then takes Congress' vague policy mandate and makes the detailed decisions necessary to translate the legislation into operating programs. The implementation and operation of the programs by the agencies irritate some constituents and suggest opportunities for profit to others. These aggrieved and/or hopeful constituents then appeal to their congressman to intervene in their behalf with the bureaucratic powers that be. The system is connected when congressmen decry bureaucratic excesses and red tape while riding a grateful electorate to ever more impressive electoral showings.

Thus congressmen appropriate all the public credit generated in the system, while the bureaucracy absorbs all the costs. The bureaucrats may not enjoy their status as objects of public opprobrium, but so long as they accommodate congressmen larger budgets and grants of authority will be forthcoming. All of Washington prospers as ever larger cadres of bureaucrats promulgate ever more numerous regulations and spend ever more money. Meanwhile, ever fewer congressmen meet electoral defeat. This is the Washington system.

What should we think of such a system, beyond the trace of disillusionment we always feel upon finding that childhood ideals are not reflected in political reality? There are three recognizably distinct reactions to my description of the Washington system: (1) the cynical reaction that runs through the pages of this book, (2) a more optimistic reaction that looks at the bright side of the system, (3) an alarmist reaction that holds that the Washington system will evolve into something worse. Let us take these in order.

The Cynical View

Congressmen actively exploit the bureaucracy and the citizenry. The bureaucracy passively exploits Congress and the people. And the people? They are put in a position of attempting futilely to exploit each other. There is a difference between exchange and exploitation. People do receive services from their congressmen, and in return they provide votes. But when grateful constituents reelect their congressmen, they fail to realize that they are helping to perpetuate a system which subordinates the content of public policy to the desires of congressmen to obtain special credits with which to impress their districts. (More on this below.)

The recent campaigns provide indications that the exploitive character of the Washington system is becoming recognized. First, increasing numbers of citizens have turned to "outsider" political candidates. These citizens are only vaguely aware of what is wrong, but increasingly they feel that something is and that the source of the problem is Washington, D.C. Second, consider the suspicion and/or opposition of the "liberal establishment" to such candidates as Carter, Brown, and other new Democrats. The liberal establishment is a subset of the Washington establishment (as is the conservative establishment, to some extent). In addition to liberal bureaucrats themselves, private consultants, faculty members at prestigious eastern universities, innumerable lawyers, and their associates in the media all fatten off the Washington system. Threats to bypass or eliminate the existing channels are threats to the very existence of the Washington system. The opposition of the Washington establishment to Jimmy Carter stems not from fundamental policy differences; it stems from a real fear that some exploiters might switch positions with some exploitees.

In the end, though, all politics is exploitive. What else is new? I am most cynical about the operation of the Washington system for a second, more serious reason. Public policy emerges from the system almost as an afterthought. The shape of policy is a by-product of the way the system operates, rather than a consciously directed effort to deal with social and economic problems. Congressmen know that the specific impact of broad national policies on their districts is difficult to see, that effects are hidden, so to speak. They know too that individual congressmen are not held responsible for the collective outcome produced by 535 members of Congress. Thus, in order to attain reelection, congressmen focus on things that are both more recognizable in their impact and more credible indicators of the individual congressman's power—federal projects and individual favors for constituents. In order to purchase a steady flow of the latter, congressmen trade away less valuable currency—their views on public policy. The typical public law is simply the outcome of enough individual bargains to build a majority. Maybe that's just politics, but we don't have to like it, and political scientists need not construct silly defenses for it.

The existence of the Washington system locks us into the New Deal way of doing things: pass a law, appropriate a lot of money, and establish a new federal bureaucracy. No reasoned analysis underlies that method of operation. The electoral interest of incumbent congressmen does. Critics used to complain that we had a nineteenth-century Congress in a twentieth-century world. Things have improved a bit: we now have a 1930s Congress in a 1970s world. During the primaries in the spring of 1976 I listened with amusement as the media echoed the congressional contenders' charges that Carter was not specific on the issues. Never did the media stop to ponder whether the congressional contenders might be specific but mindless. Prior to Carter's move into the mainstream of the Democratic party, he was in fact the only genuine hope for radical policy change. The congressional contenders were the true conservatives despite their talk of federal activism. They had in mind only one type of activism: centralized federal programs whose primary effect would be to enrich the electoral coalitions that regularly return them to office.

The Washington system stifles genuine policy innovation. In recent years we have heard talk about more flexible, less centralized policies involving moves away from large federal bureaucracies. We should expect more talk but little action in the near future despite Jimmy Carter's intentions. To lessen federal control over the daily operation of the country is to lessen incumbent congressmen's chances of reelection. So their voluntary cooperation is not likely. Consider, for example, the revenue-sharing program, whose extension in 1976 encountered serious congressional difficulties. Representative Barber Conable (R., New York) identified four sources of opposition. The first includes those philosophically opposed to separation of the taxing and spending powers. The other three facets of the opposition are, in Conable's words:

2) A related group of power brokers, centered in our Appropriations Committee, who don't like any program over which they don't have direct and detailed control. Revenue sharing money doesn't have many federal strings tied on it, is automatically appropriated and automatically distributed, which makes it low priority money for those who want to throw their weight around in the distribution process.

3) Those congressional grumps who felt they didn't get much credit for the program, the benefits of which showed up in the local real estate tax rate and thus helped reelect local officials rather than congressmen.

4) Those grantsmen with political clout nationally, who because of their leverage with Congress and bureaucracy feel that they will do better than the average with selective categorical grants, and so don't want to see available community money watered down for them by automatic distribution to communities too weak to be good at grantsmanship.[1]

Even granting that Conable is a Republican and favorably disposed to revenue sharing, his analysis is plausible and suggests the difficulties likely to be faced by programs not cast from the traditional (i.e. New Deal) mold. Professor Harold Seidman, a more disinterested observer, provides a similar, if more general perspective:

Decentralization makes an excellent theme for campaign speeches, but those who take campaign promises seriously run the risk of incurring congressional displeasure. Governors and mayors are competitors of Senators and Representatives. Once decisions are made outside of the Nation's capital, local officials can deal directly with Federal field staff and members of Congress are excluded from a key role in the decision-making processes. Constituents do not have to come to their congressman for assistance. What is worse, a local official may announce a Federal project or grant before the congressman can issue his press release.[2]

Even the reorganization of the federal bureaucracy in an attempt to improve efficiency generates little or no support among congressmen. When Richard Nixon proposed a large-scale cabinet reorganization and consolidation, the fate of the proposal could be read from the faces of the listening committee and subcommittee chairmen. No chance. Democratic opposition to a Republican president? Not at all. I doubt that Jimmy Carter will fare any better. In the first flush of victory congressional leaders may voice support for reorganization in the abstract. Whether 250-odd House and Senate subcommittee chairmen will support a specific reorganization plan is a far different matter. Subgovernments built up over the years are potential victims of any federal reorganization, and few congressmen will sacrifice their smoothly operating subgovernment in order to help create a more smoothly operating government.

This, then, is the basis of the cynical view of the Washington system. The incentives of incumbent congressmen lead them to protect and encourage the structure and operation of a centralized bureaucratic state almost irrespective of the kind of public policy that constrains our present and shapes our future.

The Optimistic View

In district A I spoke to a Democratic state legislator who represents one of the most solidly Republican areas in the congressional district. "How do you do it?" I asked. He told me that although nominally a part-time politician, he spends seventy-eighty hours a week on political matters. During a biweekly radio spot he discusses legislative business and also announces his forthcoming schedule. A sample:

> On Monday night from 6:00 to 10:00 p.m. I will be at the fire station in Johnsburg. At the same time Tuesday night I will be at the post office in Pearsville. At the same time Wednesday night I will be at the Elks in Dovertown, etc. Come on out and talk. Tell me what problems you have. Maybe I can help you.

He went on to argue that more people know him than know the congressman or senator, because car registrations and student loans touch people more directly than matters of national policy. While talking to me he thought he sensed disapproval or at least lack of admiration for his activities. He grew agitated.

> You've got to understand. The little guy just can't get through the bureaucracy. He can't get anything done. They —— him over all the time. What a state representative can do is to protect the little guy and help the little guy. That's what you do to get reelected. That's the job of the elected official today.

The optimistic view of the Washington system generalizes the sentiments expressed by the state legislator. One can argue that in a complex, post industrial society big business, big labor, and big government must be accepted as givens. And given that the bureaucracy exists and will continue to exist, a critical need for ombudsman services exists and will continue to exist. So, instead of lamenting the decline of Congress as a policymaking body, we should rejoice in the vigor and effectiveness shown by contemporary congressmen in their ombudsman role. Somehow we have muddled through again as we have in the past. Our institutions have adapted themselves to the changing needs of the society.

Certainly the optimistic view contains an element of truth. Ombudsman services are needed, and congressmen do the job well. Congressmen, not surprisingly, are partial toward the optimistic view. One of Clapp's subjects observes:

> One reason we get the mail is because people either have not been able to find out with whom they should deal or have been

exposed to a lot of red tape. The federal government is entering into the lives of people more and more, and the agencies are not known to them or are not near. Thus they think of their congressman. One of the most rewarding things we do is rectifying some of the erroneous decisions or lack of attention from administrative agencies to the problems of individual constituents. In many instances the executive branch is wrong, and the only recourse the individual has is to come to a senator or member of the House.[3]

Basically the optimistic view differs from the cynical view in two respects. First, it treats incumbent congressman as much more innocent than the cynical view. Incumbents are just public-spirited good ol' boys protecting their constituents from the ravages of the bureaucracy. Certainly they are not compounding the problem. Second, the optimistic view holds ombudsman activities in sufficiently high regard that it accepts the decline of the programmatic role of congressmen and Congress as a fair exchange or else considers that decline a reflection of an inevitable growth of executive dominance.

The optimistic view embodies an alternative explanation for the events and processes about which I have written. Perhaps it is the more correct explanation. If so, we could all sleep more easily.

The Alarmist View

I wish I could write that the alarmist view is merely the ultimate absurd extension of the cynical view. Unfortunately, not only do some reasonable (at least intelligent, if sometimes unreasonable) observers hold that view, but I can point to enough suggestive examples that I would hesitate to dismiss the alarmist view out of hand. The argument runs like this.

What began as harmless or even beneficial dabbling in bureaucratic affairs has become (or threatens to become) congressional addiction to the bureaucratic "fix." Each of the preceding two views presumes that congressmen have the upper hand in dealing with the bureaucracy. Do they? Will they always? As the federal role grows larger and larger, as more and more citizens are directly affected by bureaucratic decisions, will the bureaucracy come to dominate the Congress–bureaucracy relationship, at least on significant decisions? Will we reach a state in which the Congress becomes so dependent on the constituency service function that the bureaucracy has make-or-break power over congressmen or at least the ability to inflict great political pain and suffering?

Worrisome examples are easy to cite. When certain congressmen made noises about reducing the operating subsidies of Amtrak, the latter responded by unveiling plans for reduced operations. Just coincidentally, lines to be eliminated seemed to run through the districts of critical members of the Appropriations and Commerce committees. Just coincidence, of course, and no irrevocable decision had been reached. Amtrak just wanted Congress to know the lines along which it was thinking.[4]

Similarly, the congressman who threatens to rock the boat may find that a base, veterans' hospital, or important government program in his district is under consideration for possible elimination or termination. The story is an old one. When a school budget gets cut, the head bureaucrats announce that 2,000 classroom teachers must be released, or the football program will be eliminated. For some reason guidance counselors, deputy assistant principals, and other clerks are indispensable. Similarly, when city budgets are cut, firemen and on-the-beat policeman stand in danger of loss of employment. Apparently the city would shut down if any middling-level clerical jobs were eliminated. Bureaucrats are not without weapons in their struggles against elected officials, and the more the elected officials come to rely on favors from the bureaucrats, the more vulnerable they are to the cessation of those favors. He who lives by the boondoggle may die by it as well.

As one would expect, incumbent congressmen are aware of their growing vulnerability to bureaucratic decisions. Presumably they will search for ways to lessen that vulnerability. For example, during the defense appropriations debate of April 1976, House Majority Leader Tip O'Neill offered an amendment to prohibit the Department of Defense from reducing operations at any domestic military base by more than 50 percent unless Congress had been notified prior to March 15, 1973. This intriguing amendment would have given Congress a veto over the closing of any domestic military base (including 160 already targeted for closure or cutback by the Ford administration). The amendment failed, 152–202. During the debate Richard Ichord (D., Missouri) charged that "this amendment would require the operation of our defense forces not for the primary purpose of defending the United States, but for the economic concerns of local, self-serving interests." Apparently 152 congressmen approved of the latter point of view. On May 7, 1976, a weaker O'Neill amendment passed. This one provided that Congress should receive one year's notice prior to the closing or major cutback of any domestic military installation.[5]

In addition to such imaginative safeguards, congressmen can retaliate against uppity bureaucrats. The appropriations process is an annual event, and new program authorizations are constantly sought. But congressmen must stand for reelection every two years. A defeated congressman receives little solace from the knowledge that his buddies will avenge his defeat someday. Thus the better part of valor might simply involve no attempts to frustrate bureaucratic plans. Individual congressmen might find it much safer to accept the crumbs thrown to them by the bureaucracy and otherwise just not get in the way. They could continue to be congressmen, but real power would have passed to the hands of an appointive, self-perpetuating coterie of career officials.

The Three Views: Alternatives or a Developmental Sequence?

I do not consider the three viewpoints on the Washington system as mutually exclusive. Rather, I think they are views one might form by examining the system at three different points in time. In the early 1960s I suspect that most observers would have agreed upon the optimistic view. In the mid-seventies I believe that we are well into the cynical view. At some unspecified future time will the alarmist view constitute an accurate description rather than a discomforting scenario?

A Fourth View: Kill the Messenger

Before concluding this chapter I wish to mention a fourth viewpoint held by some doctrinaire liberals, particularly those doing well under the existing system. This viewpoint does not focus primarily on the Washington system itself; rather, it focuses on the motives of those who attack that system. Consider the following remarks (from a speech printed in the *Los Angeles Times*) by Vernon Jordan, executive director of the Urban League:

> In a few brief years our nation has moved from "we shall overcome" to "we don't care." That is the real meaning of the anti-Washington rhetoric we've been hearing in this presidential campaign. Cutting across the ideological spectrum and afflicting liberals and conservatives alike, it preaches a doctrine I call "The New Minimalism"—meaning less government, less spending, less federal manpower and less government regulation.
>
> Somehow, in their calculations, the New Minimalists don't include fat Pentagon budgets or tax expenditures that benefit the well-off. They ignore the fact that *less government means less protection for people without resources; that less spending means fewer desperately needed social programs and stark hunger for those in poverty; that fewer government employees means fewer public services; that less government regulation means an end to civil-rights enforcement.* (My emphasis)[6]

Jordan's constituency has suffered horribly at the hands of white majority government in this country. Thus upon reading his attack any liberal Democrat feels a twinge of panic; there is an immediate temptation to search one's soul for a trace of racism or at least insensitivity to the plight of the have-nots in our society. Such temptations should be resisted, and Jordan's arguments should be recognized for what they are: nonsense.

To condemn the Washington system is not to say that we need less government or less humanistic government. It is simply to recognize that the present government has pathological aspects. What we do need is better government: more efficient, more flexible, and more creative government. If we had better government we could use existing levels of input to provide higher levels of services or lower levels of input to maintain existing levels of services. Naturally those interests faring well under the present system may hesitate to gamble on the chance of something better. But despite sympathy with their cause, we should not let them bully us into believing that we now live in the best of all possible worlds. All of this country's goodness, truth, and beauty does not dwell in the hearts of those who work in Washington, D.C.

Chapter 9
What Lies Ahead?

The Washington system grew up as the public sector expanded. At first the system was an unforeseen by-product of genuine attempts to legislate in the general interests of the American citizenry. Today the system has become an end in itself. It enables congressmen and bureaucrats to achieve their most dearly held goals by giving the appearance of satisfying the goals of the American people. In reality, public policy in this country is hostage to the personal goals of congressmen and the bureaucracy.

What lies ahead? Will the system continue to operate as presently or even degenerate into the bureaucratic state conjured up by alarmists (chapter 8)? Or can we expect or hope for more favorable developments? My personal viewpoint is pessimistic. I see little chance of any major changes in the operation of the Washington system, at least in the short term. The system is a response to people's incentives, and I do not see any potential sources of comparably strong incentives for change.

Congressmen, first of all, will not voluntarily acquiesce in the dismantling of the system. Congress embraces those reforms which advance the interests of its members and rejects most others. Even those congressmen who might win office by running against the system will find themselves subject to its temptations once they arrive in Washington.

Nor will the bureaucracy disrupt the operations of the system by ceasing to accommodate congressmen. To do so would invite great pain and suffering at the hands of frustrated congressmen. Besides, the bureaucracy thrives under the system. Why on earth would it try to bring about change?

And the people? What is our incentive to change? Would we voluntarily give up our particular plums? Hardly. Each group in the population favors disconnecting the Washington system by elimination and reorganization of agencies and programs not related to its special preserve: "Let's you and him do away with the Washington system. My program is in the public interest."

Not only does each group in the population wish to maintain the status quo on matters relating to it, while changing it on matters relating to others, but, additionally, each group fights harder to preserve those programs from which it benefits than to eliminate or modify those programs from which it doesn't.[1] And given the way congressmen respond, the result is no change. We hear much talk about the seeming immortality of bureaucracies. Professor Herbert Kaufman, for example, recently published a short study on this topic.[2] He finds that of 175 organizational units existing in 1923—half a century ago—148 of them still existed in 1973. And 246 new ones had grown up. But bureaucracies are not immortal; they are in fact weak. They achieve the appearance of immortality by building constituencies who scream to their congressmen when their agencies or their agencies' programs are endangered. *Bureaucracies are immortal only insofar as Congress grants them immortality.* And Congress bestows such grants only so long as congressmen can use the bureaucracies. And congressmen can use the bureaucracies only because we, the people, pay them in votes to use the bureaucracies. The enemy is us.

What of the currently popular "sunset laws?" These laws provide for automatic review of every agency or program after a specified interval of time. The laws carry a presumption of guilt: without positive action to extend the program or recharter the agency existence ceases. Does the current popularity of such laws (fifty-one co-sponsors in the U.S. Senate) contradict what I have just written? Not really.

Those threatened by the elimination of an agency or program fight harder than those with a generalized interest in efficiency or cost-cutting. Thus the renewal process will be dominated by those with a material stake in preserving agencies and programs. Besides, consider the real import of the sunset laws: congressmen gain life and death power over every federal agency and program. In theory Congress has that power now, but it is a blunderbuss power, difficult to use. Ah, but when agencies and programs automatically die every five years, say, the use of that power becomes easier and the threat of it more credible. Rather than attempt positive action to eliminate a program, an unhappy congressman can quietly let it be known that he will not lift a finger to keep a program from dying. The sunset laws might prevent the present Washington system from degenerating into the bureaucratic state feared by the alarmists, but such laws will not upset the Washington system. To the contrary, *they will enhance the power of individual congressmen to extort constituency favors from the federal bureaucracy.* Even so, one should note that such proposals have received a more favorable reception in the Senate, a body more media-oriented, issue-oriented (and presidency-oriented) than the House. The representatives see little reason to tinker with a system that works very well for them already. In fact, members of the House were even somewhat leery of adopting President Ford's weak proposals for the reform of federal regulatory commissions and policies. The system works beautifully from their standpoint. Why tamper with a winner?

Although I am pessimistic, I am not absolutely so. Changes in the Washington system could arise from two different sources. But compared to the sturdy beams which hold up that system, these sources of change are fragile sticks. Probably they will not support our hopes.

First, the people could elect an outsider president committed to wholesale changes in the Washington system. (Perhaps they did so in 1976; as yet we cannot say.) If the issue became heated enough, congressmen could be forced to acquiesce in modifications of the system. On the whole congressmen achieve reelection on the basis of constituency service, not issues. But that is not to deny that on occasion an issue becomes so important that congressional positions on that issue determine the vote. Civil rights, school busing, and abortion have been such issues, although never in the nation as a whole.

As I have argued, citizens will not voluntarily consent to give up those elements of the status quo from which they profit. But a majority might vote to coerce universal abandonment of federal boondoogles. The analogy is a familiar one. People do not voluntarily contribute an extra $100 to government, but they do vote for universally applicable tax raises. Individual incentives will not support piece-by-piece disconnection of the Washington system, but they might support wholesale dismantlement. The perception of universal sacrifice is critical.

In any case, the preceding argument is a frail one. At the least, conditions in the nation would need to grow much worse than they are to give the argument any real possibilities. And even so, when the bureaucratic fur hits the fan, we might all find that we'd rather live with the present system than experience the uncertainties inherent in changing our established ways.

The Washington system could change for a second, similarly weak reason. Quite simply, congressmen themselves might get tired of it. I mentioned in chapter 1 that the voluntary retirement rate of congressmen has risen during the early 1970s. A number of factors are probably at work. Congressional pensions have improved, for one thing. But additionally, some congressmen report that holding the office is just no fun anymore. Some refer to the poisoned atmosphere of Watergate-era Washington. Other responses give us some reason to hope. Speaker Carl L. Albert, for example, told the Associated Press that:

> I think there is still a lot of personal satisfaction in serving in Congress . . .
>
> It's harder work than it used to be. There is a lot more work and there is a lot more interruptions . . .
>
> I spend a lot more hours than I used to on the chore type of work.[3]

Another retiree, James Hastings (R., New York), told the *Washington Post* that one of his job frustrations was that his constituents didn't care about his legislative accomplishments:

> In the minds of many people those things don't count. Number one they are not aware of them. And number two, what's important is what I can do for them on a personal basis . . .
>
> All a member of Congress needs to do to win reelection is run a good public relations operation and answer his constituent mail promptly.
>
> What kind of whore am I?[4]

Perhaps such sentiments will become widespread. Perhaps we've reached a rough equilibrium between constituency service and public policymaking within the congressional workload. Beyond a certain point congressmen simply quit rather than shift any more effort from the latter to the former.

Recall that a former Republican congressman in district B implied that many members of today's Congress could not earn $45,000 a year in the public sector. Maybe he's right. But then again, as the tangible benefits of holding office increase, more capable individuals might seek the office. Such individuals might not be willing to spend their careers as errand boys. Moreover, confidence in their own capabilities could lead them to tolerate greater electoral risks than present incumbents. Defeat would not mean teaching school, selling insurance, or drawing up wills back in Possum Hollow.

I suspect there is too much optimism in the preceding paragraphs. But where else can we place our hopes? United States congressmen gave us the Washington establishment. Ultimately, only they can take it away.

the small society   **by Brickman**

Distributed by Washington Star Syndicate

Appendix
*The Expansion of the Federal Role**

The American citizen is quite aware that the scope of his government has widened considerably in the past two generations. Today all of us in some way or another come into direct contact with government. Government regulations affect whom we can hire, fire, and admit to schools; what we can eat, drink, and inject; what we can buy, sell, ship, wear, and so forth. Government contracts provide business for the semiprivate sector. Government programs support jobs in the public sector. Government funds trickle down to us through various income maintenance, health, education, veterans, and other programs. Without passing judgment on the merits of any of these activities we can make the simple observation that in one way or another we all feed at the public trough.

Traditional conservatives have long denounced the expanding influence of the federal government (to be sure, they have notable blind spots where the defense and intelligence bureaucracies are concerned). In recent years, however, the audience receptive to conservative rhetoric has grown, as an increasing proportion of the middle class has come to believe that there is too much government. When the National Highway Safety Transportation Agency decrees that seat belts shall have a will of their own, or HEW proscribes mother-daughter events in local school districts, many citizens cry "enough!" Increasingly, moderates and liberals have joined conservatives in warning of a future in which our lives are governed through regulations promulgated by an unelected, unresponsive class of career bureaucrats. This growing concern has produced electoral success for antigovernment politicians such as Wallace, Reagan, and for a time Carter on the national level and various governors, e.g. "lower our expectations" Brown, on the state level. The size and scope of government promises to be a critical and continuing issue for the foreseeable future.

Whether or not we think we have too much government at present, how much government do we have, and how has it been growing? What are the facts about which we must eventually make political judgments? Let us briefly consider three indicators of the scope of the national government: employment, expenditures, and rules and regulations.

Figure A1 presents data on the growth of paid civilian employment by levels of government in the United States. In the post-World War II period we see a steady growth in the size of the federal work force but at a rate much lower than popular discussions might lead one to believe. In fact, the national population grew at a faster rate than federal employment in the postwar years. The figures do not appear to support the casual view of a gargantuan federal bureaucracy expanding at an exponential rate. Employment figures are somewhat misleading, however. Note that state and local employment *has* increased at something like an exponential rate. A fair share of this growth has been the direct result of federal policies. Federal programs encourage and even mandate that subnational units institute and carry out various activities. Federal money (categorical grants, matching funds, etc.) provides a large part of the wherewithal used to operate these programs and pay their operators. The true picture of employment caused directly or indirectly by federal programs is obtained by adding to the federal trend line a large fraction of the state and local trend.[1] This combined trend indeed shows a dramatic increase.

In the post-World War II years federal spending increased, of course, although at a rate not much higher than the rate of growth of GNP.[2] Again, state and local expenditures increased at a much faster rate, more than twice as fast, in fact. And again, we must note that much of the state and local increase stems from federally mandated or otherwise encouraged programs for which local and state governments must share the cost (the current property tax rebellions reflect the federal chickens coming home to roost). Figure A2 illustrates the recent growth of federal expenditures. Also graphed is the varying defense portion of federal expenditures. Evidently, beginning in about the mid-1950s, the defense *share* of the federal budget began to decline. This relative decline was greatest between 1955 and

Figure A1. The Growth of Government: Paid Civilian Employment

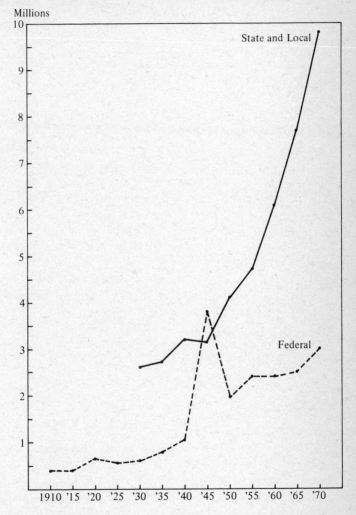

Source: U.S. Bureau of the Census, *Historical Statistics of the United States,* Series Y-308, Y-332.

Figure A2. The Growth of Federal Expenditures: Total and National Defense

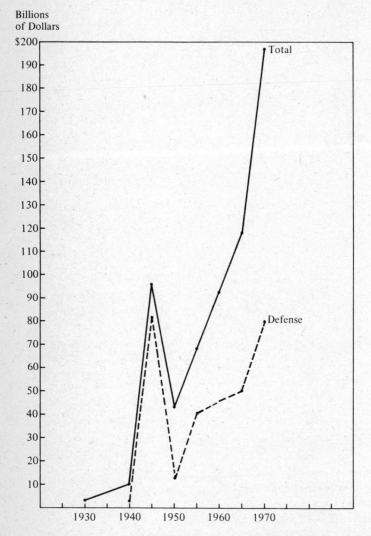

Source: U.S. Bureau of the Census, Historical Statistics, Series Y-340, Y-473.

1965 but stopped under the impact of Vietnam. What was taking up the slack produced by the declining share of defense during this period? Figure A3 provides some answers.

Beginning in the late 1940s federal income security expenditures began to grow at a rate which in retrospect appears approximately exponential. These expenditures fund programs dealing with retirement and disability payments, unemployment compensation, public assistance programs of various types, and the broad category of programs under the heading of social services. In 1955 expenditures for such purposes amounted to less than one-quarter of the defense budget. By 1970 they were more than half as large. Figure A3 shows the rapid growth in "Great Society" health and education programs, as well as veterans expenditures in the wake of Vietnam.

In sum, the expenditure data must be broken down to reveal the true picture. Since Dwight D. Eisenhower took office, federal expenditures have increased by a factor of five or six; domestic expenditures have increased by a factor of more than fifteen. Possibly every dollar spent has produced a corresponding return in human happiness. Traditional liberals might say yes, traditional conservatives no.[3] But in any case the programs instituted, the jobs created, and the dollars spent have cost incumbent congressmen nothing, while they have produced great increases in their happiness. From the standpoint of the American taxpayer the benefit–cost ratio of federal programs is a subject of legitimate political debate. For our congressmen, however, the matter is unambiguous. Establish a federal program, fund it, then help constituents get as much as they can get out of it.

In a sense the preceding discussion of federal jobs and federal expenditures does not address the most critical issue. Americans generally favor high employment policies, and they do not appear to threaten imminent revolt over the federal income tax. If federal employees only dammed rivers, built mass transit systems, caught criminals, and delivered other tangible services, I doubt that the current antigovernment, anti-Washington feeling would exist. But increased federal jobs and expenditures are only symptomatic of something more fundamental: the growing regulatory role of the federal government. An increasing number of Americans resent government not because they are satiated with tangible goods and

Figure A3. The Growth of Government: Federal Spending in Selected Domestic Areas

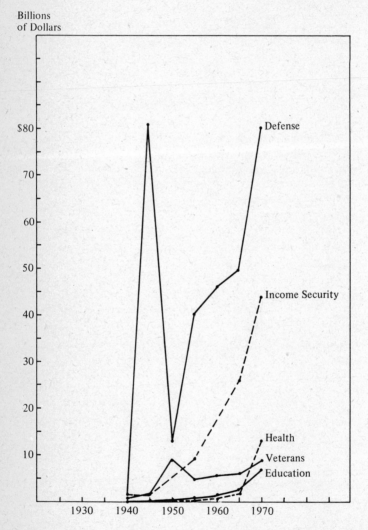

Billions
of Dollars

$80

70

60

50

40

30

20

10

Defense

Income Security

Health

Veterans

Education

1930   1940   1950   1960   1970

Source: U.S. Bureau of the Census, *Historical Statistics,* Series Y-476, Y-479.

services, but because they perceive government as too often engaged in regulating their behavior—telling them to do things they otherwise would not do or to refrain from doing things they otherwise would.

Perhaps the most striking commentary on the increasing regulatory role of the federal government is provided by a perusal of the *Federal Register*. This publication of the General Services Administration contains updates of the various rules, regulations, and legal notices emanating from the executive branch of the government. Table A1 contains a simple statistic: the number of pages in selected years of the *Federal Register*. The figures in the table tell an important story. Not until the mid-1960s did the federal bureaucracy push its activity levels back to the point reached during the years of national mobilization. But, in the decade since, the sheer number of pages devoted to bureaucratic promulgations expanded fourfold.[4] No doubt this underestimates the increasing regulatory impact on the average citizen, for the increase in regulations stems from domestic bureaucracies promulgating in the areas of health, education, hiring, consuming, safety, and other areas closer to everyday lives than previous targets of government regulation.

The summary picture is this: one citizen is currently employed in the public sector for every four citizens employed in the private sector. Government expenditures now amount to more than 40 percent of national income. Bureaucracies daily seek new areas of our lives to regulate.

Are we better off because of all this activity, or are we worse off? The question is terribly difficult. In fact, it actually has no theoretical answer. But of one thing we can be sure. The United States Congress is responsible for these levels of activity, and United States congressmen are better off because of them.

Table A1. Pages Contained in Selected Years of the *Federal Register*

1936	2,355
1946	14,736
1956	10,528
1966	16,850
1975	60,221

Notes

Introduction

1. Actually this strategy appears new only on the presidential level; congressmen have been following it for years. See Richard Fenno, "If, As Ralph Nader Says, Congress Is 'the Broken Branch,' How Come We Love Our Congressmen So Much?" in Norman Ornstein, ed., *Congress in Change* (New York: Praeger, 1975), pp. 277–87.

2. Some psychologists might reply that the mass public "needs" conspiratorial explanations—that ordinary citizens are incapable of comprehending a complex political reality. I disagree. Our citizens and our politicians have been the subjects of too much psychological analysis in recent years. We would do well to focus on the simple, objective explanations for political reactions and events, rather than to seize upon romantic, imaginative, but typically fictitious psychological theories. Compare, for example, the explanations of McCarthyism propounded by sociologists in Daniel Bell, ed., *The Radical Right* (New York: Doubleday, 1964), with those advanced by political scientists such as Nelson Polsby in "Toward an Explanation of McCarthyism," *Political Studies* (1960), pp. 250–71.

Chapter 1

1. For analyses of the myths and realities surrounding the seniority system see Raymond Wolfinger and Joan Hollinger, "Safe Seats, Seniority, and Power in Congress," in Robert Peabody and Nelson Polsby, eds., *New Perspectives on the House of Representatives,* 2d ed. (Chicago: Rand McNally, 1969), pp. 55–77; Barbara Hinckley, *The Seniority System in Congress* (Bloomington: Indiana University Press, 1971).

2. The figures for the House are a bit on the high side of 90 percent, while those for the Senate are a bit on the low side. See Charles Jones, *Every Second Year* (Washington, D.C.: Brookings Institution, 1967); Warren Kostroski, "Party and Incumbency in Post-War Senate Elections: Trends, Patterns, and Models," *American Political Science Review* 68 (1973): 1213–34.

3. Morris P. Fiorina, David W. Rohde, and Peter Wissel, "Historical Change in House Turnover" in Ornstein, ed., *Congress in Change,* pp. 24–57; H. Douglas Price, "Congress and the Evolution of Legislative 'Professionalism'", ibid., pp. 2–23; Nelson Polsby, "The Institutionalization of the U.S. House of Representatives," *American Political Science Review* 62 (1968): 144–68.

4. James S. Young, *The Washington Community* (New York: Harcourt, Brace and World, 1966).

5. For those unfamiliar with the details of the 1909–11 revolt, some general background might be helpful. In the decades following the Civil War, a succession of strong speakers (in both parties) including Blaine, Randall, Keifer, Carlisle,

"Czar" Reed, and "Boss" Cannon centralized power in the office of the Speaker. Their power rested on such tangibles as control of the committee assignment process, the power of recognition, and dominance of the Rules Committee, and perhaps on such intangibles as ideological support for strong party government. Speaker Cannon (1903-11) pushed the powers of his office to their utmost at a time when members of the House were increasingly less willing to accept arbitrary leadership. Cannon ruthlessly manipulated committee assignments and other formal powers to whip his party into line behind the program of the "regular" wing of the party. Eventually time ran out on him. The 1908 election weakened the regular wing of the party and strengthened the "progressive" wing, and in 1909 a loose coalition of progressive Republicans and Democrats managed to circumscribe the Speaker's heretofore unlimited right of recognition. In 1910 the same coalition struck a major blow expanding the Rules Committee, removing the Speaker from it, and giving to the House as a whole the power to select the members of the committee. Later that year the Democrats won control of the House and, in organizing the Congress in 1911, gave to the House as a whole the power to assign its members to committees. Seniority soon became an automatic, nearly inviolable rule for choosing the committee leadership. The net result of the revolt was to give to the rank-and-file membership of Congress the ability to shape their own political futures. No longer could they be forced to cast a vote that might cripple them in their district; no longer could their internal base of influence be removed at the displeasure of the Speaker. The modern House—a decentralized body of career politicians answerable only to their districts—dates from the events of 1909-11. For more extended discussions see Charles Jones, "Joseph G. Cannon and Howard W. Smith: An Essay on the Limits of Leadership in the House of Representatives," *Journal of Politics* 30 (1968): 617-46; Nelson Polsby, Miriam Gallagher, and Barry Rundquist, "The Growth of the Seniority System in the U.S. House of Representatives," *American Political Science Review* 63 (1969): 787-807; Kenneth Shepsle, *The Giant Jigsaw Puzzle: Democratic Committee Assignments in the Modern House,* forthcoming.

6. David Mayhew, "Congressional Elections: The Case of the Vanishing Marginals," *Polity* 6 (1974): 295-317.

7. In the most recent election unofficial returns indicate a continuation of these trends. Only thirteen incumbents went down to defeat. Using the 55 percent rule of thumb, over 80 percent of the 1976 winners would be classified as safe, including fifty-four of the seventy-eight-person Democratic "Watergate class" who sought reelection.

Chapter 2

1. For a more extended discussion of marginal districts see Morris P. Fiorina, *Representatives, Roll Calls, and Constituencies* (Lexington, Mass.: D.C. Heath, 1974), passim.

2. Herbert Asher and Herbert Weisberg, "Congressional Voting Change: A Longitudinal Study of Voting on Selected Issues," paper delivered at the annual meeting of the American Political Science Association, San Francisco, 1975.

3. These data are drawn from Fiorina, *Representatives, Roll Calls, and Constituencies,* chap. 5.

4. Ibid.

Chapter 3

1. On religion in 1960 see Philip Converse, "Religion and Politics: the 1960 Election," in Angus Campbell et al., *Elections and the Political Order* (New York: Wiley, 1966), pp. 96-124. On the New Deal cleavages in 1964 and race throughout the 1960s see Gerald Pomper, *Voters' Choice* (New York: Dodd, Mead, 1975).

2. In 1962 the Supreme Court handed down the original "one man, one vote" decision in Baker v. Carr. This decision struck down the Tennessee apportionment for the state legislature on the ground that it violated the equal protection clause of the Fourteenth Amendment. The court extended its decision to Congress in Wesberry v. Sanders in 1964.

3. Edward R. Tufte, "The Relationship between Seats and Votes in Two-Party Systems," *American Political Science Review* 67 (1973): 540-54; idem, "Communication," *American Political Science Review* 68 (1974): 211-13.

4. John A. Ferejohn, "On the Decline in Competition in Congressional Elections," *American Political Science Review,* forthcoming, July 1977.

5. Charles Bullock, "Redistricting and Congressional Stability, 1962-1972," *Journal of Politics* 37 (1975): 569-75. Albert Cover, "One Good Term Deserves Another: The Advantage of Incumbency in Congressional Elections," paper delivered at the annual meeting of the American Political Science Association, Chicago, 1976.

6. Robert S. Erikson, "The Advantage of Incumbency in Congressional Elections," *Polity* 3 (1971): 395-405; idem, "Malapportionment, Gerrymandering, and Party Fortunes in Congressional Elections," *American Political Science Review* 66 (1972): 1234-1355.

7. Donald Stokes and Warren Miller, "Party Government and the Saliency of Congress," *Public Opinion Quarterly* 26 (1962): 531-46.

8. Angus Campbell et al., *The American Voter* (New York: Wiley, 1960).

9. Stokes and Miller, "Party Government and the Saliency of Congress."

10. Norman Vie, Sidney Verba, and John Petrocik, *The Changing American Voter* (Cambridge, Mass.: Harvard University Press, 1976).

11. Kevin Phillips, *The Emerging Republican Majority* (New York: Anchor, 1970); Walter Burnham, *Critical Elections and the Mainsprings of American Politics* (New York: Norton, 1970).

12. Walter D. Burnham and William Chambers, eds., "Party Systems and the Political Process," *The American Party Systems,* 2d ed. (New York: Oxford, 1975), pp. 308-57; Erikson, "Malapportionment, Gerrymandering, and Party Fortunes in Congressional Elections"; Ferejohn, "On the Decline of Competition in Congressional Elections."

13. Arthur Miller, "Political Issues and Trust in Government: 1964-1970," *American Political Science Review* 68 (1974): 951-72.

14. U.S. Congress, Senate, Committee on Government Operations, "Confi-

dence and Concern: Citizens View American Government," Dec. 3, 1973, Hearing.

15. Kostroski, "Party and Incumbency in Post-War Senate Elections."

Chapter 5

1. Henry David Thoreau, *Walden* (London: Walter Scott Publishing Co., no date) p. 72.

2. For a more extended discussion of the electoral motivation see Fiorina, *Representatives, Roll Calls, and Constituencies,* chap. 2; David R. Mayhew, *Congress: The Electoral Connection* (New Haven: Yale University Press, 1974).

3. For a discussion of the goals of bureaucrats see William Niskanen, *Bureaucracy and Representative Government* (Chicago: Aldine-Atherton, 1971).

4. The traditional pork barrel is the subject of an excellent treatment by John Ferejohn. See his *Pork Barrel Politics: Rivers and Harbors Legislation, 1947-1968* (Stanford: Stanford University Press, 1974).

5. Charles Clapp, *The Congressman: His Job As He Sees It* (Washington: Brookings Institution, 1963), p. 84.

6. Richard Fenno, *The Power of The Purse* (Boston: Little, Brown, 1966); Aaron Wildavsky, *The Politics of the Budgetary Process,* 2d ed. (Boston: Little, Brown, 1974).

7. Clapp, *The Congressman: His Job As He Sees It,* p. 84.

8. "Hays Improves Rapidly From Overdose," *Los Angeles Times,* June 12, 1976, part I, p. 19. Similarly, Congressman Robert Leggett (D., Calif.) won re-election in 1976 even amid revelations of a thirteen-year bigamous relationship and rumors of other affairs and improprieties. The *Los Angeles Times* wrote:

> Because of federal spending, times are good here in California's 4th Congressional District, and that is a major reason why local political leaders in both parties, as well as the man on the street, believe that Leggett will still be their congressman next year. . . .
>
> Leggett has concentrated on bringing federal dollars to his district and on acting as an ombudsman for constituents having problems with their military pay or Social Security or GI benefit checks. He sends out form letters to parents of newborn children congratulating them.

Traditionally, personal misbehavior has been one of the few shoals on which incumbent congressmen could founder. But today's incumbents have so entrenched themselves by personal service to constituents that even scandal does not harm them mortally. See David Johnson, "Rep. Leggett Expected to Survive Sex Scandal," *Los Angeles Times,* July 26, 1976, part I, p. 1.

9. See the appendix for data on the growth of the executive branch, particularly table A1, which provides a rough picture of the striking increase in bureaucratic rules and regulations that have the force of law.

10. Clapp, *The Congressman: His Job As He Sees It,* p. 94.

Chapter 6

1. Richard Fenno, "Congressmen in Their Constituencies: An Exploration," *American Political Science Review,* forthcoming.
2. Ibid.

Chapter 7

1. At the time of this writing (94th Congress) only seven congressmen reported that their district offices were not open while they were in Washington. The seven were Evins (Democrat) of Tennessee, elected in 1946, Jones (Democrat) of Alabama, elected in 1946, Mahon (Democrat) of Texas, elected in 1934, Sikes (Democrat) of Florida, elected in 1944, Stevens (Democrat) of Georgia, elected in 1960, Teague (Democrat) of Texas, elected in 1946, and Waggoner (Democrat) of Louisiana, elected in 1961. Note that these holdouts were exclusively southern Democrats and generally senior (five of seven elected before 1950). It is perhaps worth pointing out that three (Jones, Teague, and Mahon) were committee chairmen, and a fourth (Waggoner) has served in the elective leadership (caucus chairman). Given these internal responsibilities they might be expected to operate large district staff operations to take up the slack. Apparently, though, they didn't do it in the 1940s so don't intend to start now. In Fenno's terms they continue to follow homestyles established in a simpler era.
2. Kenneth Olson, "The Service Function of the United States Congress," in *Congress: The First Branch of Government,* (Washington: American Enterprise Institute, 1966), p. 344.
3. For additional data and discussion see Cover, "One Good Term Deserves Another."
4. *How To Succeed in Politics* (New York: McFadden Books, 1964), p. 20.
5. Norman Ornstein, "Causes and Consequences of Congressional Change: Subcommittee Reforms in the House of Representatives," in Ornstein, ed., *Congress in Change,* pp. 88–114.
6. Douglas Cater, *Power in Washington* (New York: Random House, 1964); Ernest Griffith, *Congress: Its Contemporary Role* (New York: New York University Press, 1961); Eugene Eidenberg and Roy Morey, *An Act of Congress* (New York: Norton, 1969).
7. Randall Ripley, *Congress: Process and Policy* (New York: Norton, 1975), pp. 251–52.
8. Kenneth Shepsle, "The Giant Jigsaw Puzzle: Democratic Committee Assignments in the House of Representatives." Manuscript.
9. For background discussion see G. R. Pipe, "Congressional Liaison: The Executive Branch Consolidates Its Relations with Congress," *Public Administration Review* 26 (1966): 14–24.
10. Edward de Grazia, "Congressional Liaison—An Inquiry into Its Meaning for Congress," in *Congress: The First Branch,* p. 315.
11. Ibid., p. 314.

12. Randall Ripley, *Party Leaders in the House of Representatives* (Washington, D.C.: Brookings Institution, 1967).

Chapter 8

1. Representative Barber Conable, *Washington Report,* March 9, 1976.
2. Harold Seidman, *Politics, Position and Power: The Dynamics of Federal Organization,* 2d ed. (New York: Oxford, 1975).
3. Clapp, *The Congressman: His Job As He Sees It,* p. 86.
4. Charles Peters discusses this and other examples in "Firemen First," *Washington Monthly,* March 1976, pp. 8-11. For additional background see "Amtrak Plight," *Congressional Quarterly Weekly Report,* May 29, 1976, pp. 1365-70.
5. For an accounting of the maneuverings surrounding the O'Neill amendments see *Congressional Quarterly Weekly Report,* April 17, 1976, pp. 932-33, and May 15, 1976, pp. 1161-63.
6. Vernon Jordan, " 'New Minimalism' Threatens the Poor," *Los Angeles Times,* May 6, 1976, part II, p. 7.

Chapter 9

1. An aide to Representative John Anderson, the Republican Conference Chairman, stated the problem concisely:

> If effective oversight turns up an ineffective program which results in its proposed elimination, the greatest hue and cry goes up from those with a vested interest in the program, and not from taxpayers overjoyed at the prospect of reduced federal spending.

Quoted in *Congressional Quarterly Weekly Report,* March 22, 1975, p. 595.
2. Herbert Kaufman, *Are Government Organizations Immortal?* (Washington, D.C.: Brookings Institution, 1976).
3. Quoted in *Lansing State Journal,* February 29, 1976, p. A-4.
4. Quoted in Stuart Auerbach, "Frustrated Congressman Quitting," *Washington Post,* December 27, 1975, p. A-1. Since retiring, Hastings has been convicted of operating a payroll kickback scheme in his Washington office.

Appendix

*This appendix provides the briefest of introductions to the topic. Those wishing to delve deeper might consult the following works: Roger A. Freeman, *The Growth of American Government* (Stanford: Hoover Institution, 1975); Herbert Kaufman, *Are Government Organizations Immortal?*; Martha Derthick, *Uncontrollable Spending for Social Services Grants* (Washington, D.C.: Brookings Institution, 1975).

1. The federal stimulus for the expansion of state and local government activity is widely recognized. But I am not aware of any attempts to provide precise estimates of the share of state and local activity that stems from federal sticks and carrots.

2. Interestingly, Congress paid no political penalty for extracting ever larger amounts of money from the citizenry. The increase in federal expenditures came about through an expanding economy, deficit financing, and the effects of inflation pushing people into higher tax brackets, rather than through visible, politically dangerous tax increases.

3. Currently it is fashionable to bemoan the failures of federal social programs. For a favorable assessment of the social programs of the 1960s see Sar Levitan and Robert Taggart, *The Promise of Greatness* (Cambridge, Mass.: Harvard University Press, 1976).

4. I am assuming that today's bureaucrats are no more verbose than their predecessors.

Index

Administrative Counsel of the Congress, 47
Agency for International Development, 69
Albert, Carl L., 85
American Political Science Association, 55
Army Corps of Engineers, 44

Behavioral change: of congressmen, 36–37; in electorate, 24–26, 50
Brown, Jerry, 72, 87
Bullock, Charles, 19
Bureaucracy: congressional control over, 42–43; goals of, 40; growth of, 46–49, 54, 83
Burnham, Walter, 24, 50

Carter, James, 2, 35, 72, 73, 74, 75, 87
Casework, 42–43, 44–45, 47–48. *See also* Constituency service
Cater, Douglas, 65
Civil Rights Act (*1964*), 45
Clapp, Charles, 42, 44, 47, 71
Commerce Department, 68
Conable, Barber, 74
Congress: committees, 42, 43, 64–65; professionalization of, 5–7; seniority system, 5, 6, 7, 62–63; subcommittees, 63–67
Congressional Quarterly, 13
Congressmen: advertising, 19–21, 28; allowances, 60–62; changing behavior of, 36–37; district offices, 35, 57–58; "homestyle" of, 54–55; marginal, 12–14; reelection efforts, 5, 39–40, 56, 60; resources of,

19–21, 28, 60; retirement rates, 5, 85; staff, 35, 56–60; travel allowances, 60, 61–62; turnover, 5, 6, 7, 9, 11, 54–55
Conservative Coalition Support Score, 13
Constituency service, 55, 58–60. *See also* Casework
Cover, Albert, 19

Debt limit, 70
Defense Department, 79–80
Defense Liaison Office, 68
De Grazia, Edward, 69
Democrats, 24, 48, 55, 72, 73, 75; and committee chairmanships, 63, 64; and incumbency effect, 27; vote for, 8–11, 53; voting records of, 13
Division of Labor Standards, 43

Eidenberg, Eugene, 65
Eisenhower, Dwight D., 23, 91
Electoral mandate, and marginals, 13–14
Electorate: behavioral changes in, 24–26, 50; cynicism and alienation of, 26–27
Energy policy formation, 64–65
Environmentalism, 44, 65
Erikson, Robert, 19, 24, 27, 50, 52
Establishment, Washington: alternatives to, 84–86; definition of, 2, 3; theory of, 39–49 passim; views of, 72–75

Federal government: budgets, 43, 88–92; employees, 88–89; role,